Youth Empowerment Series - Book 1

DIVINE UNION

Practicing Life With Christ in You

NEW CREATION
PRESS

Cleveland Orville McLeish MTS

ISBN: 978-1-953759-54-2 (paperback)
      978-1-953759-55-9 (eBook)

NEW CREATION
PRESS

To all future world-changers and faithful agents of change: may you create a better world for those who come after you.

To anyone who thinks there is no place for them—there is.

This book is for you.

READER'S PLEDGE

- ✓ I will live from union, not performance.
- ✓ I will test and then obey small promptings.
- ✓ I will use my words to bless, not wound.
- ✓ I will practice the presence of Jesus in ordinary places.
- ✓ I will take one Amen step each day.
- ✓ I will run my lane with grace—unshakable within.

DIVINE UNION DAILY CONFESSION

"I have been crucified with Christ; it is no longer I who live, but Christ lives in me. Today I live, speak, and serve **in His name**—in allegiance to His person, alignment with His character, and under His authority. Amen." (see Galatians 2:20 and Colossians 3:17).

BASELINE SELF-ASSESSMENT

- ✓ I start my day aware of Christ's presence.
- ✓ I test impressions with scripture and community.
- ✓ I bless with my mouth more than I complain.
- ✓ I take one "Amen step" connected to prayer each day.

TABLE OF CONTENTS

INTRODUCTION

"Christ in you, the hope of glory." — Colossians 1:27 (NKJV)

Every serious thinker in every generation asks two questions: *Who am I, and why am I here?* Followers of Jesus receive a stunning answer. Identity is no longer built from grades, likes, money, or talent. Identity is received. Christ Himself lives in you by the Holy Spirit, and His presence is both the center and the engine of your life. This book invites you to practice that reality—not as a slogan, but as a way of being.

You were made for a life that is fully human and fully alive in God. Scripture describes it as abiding: **"Abide in Me, and I in you" (John 15:4 - NASB).** Union with Christ reshapes everything—how you think, feel, decide, study, work, rest, create, and love. The gospel is more than sin management and rule-keeping. The gospel is Jesus sharing His life with you, and you learning to live from His life in you (see Galatians 2:20).

Two themes will be evident through these pages. First, the **unshakable kingdom**. Hebrews declares that in Christ we are receiving **"a kingdom which cannot be shaken." (Hebrews 12:28 - NASB)**. Young disciples need ballace. News cycles whirl, trends rise and fall, friendships change, and plans get interrupted. Stability does not come from having everything under control. Stability comes from being rooted in a King who already reigns. As that kingdom takes root within, courage, purity, generosity, and perseverance grow up from the inside out.

Second, the **still small voice** within. Jesus said, **"My sheep hear My voice, and I know them, and they follow Me." (John 10:27 - NKJV)**. Guidance is not a treasure hunt with vague clues. Guidance is a relationship with a living Lord. You will learn to notice the quiet nudges that align with scripture, to **"test all things; hold fast what is good." (1 Thessalonians 5:21 - NKJV)**, and to act with humble confidence. Discernment is not spooky or elitist. Disciples practice it in community, submit it to wise mentors, and anchor it in the Word.

This book grew out of live conversations with and observations of young adults who are hungry for both depth and practicality. The chapters transition between Biblical exposition, honest testimony, and practical applications. Spiritual life is not a split between sacred and secular. Prayer and planning belong together. Worship and homework belong together. Bodies matter, habits matter, and so do dreams and callings. The Spirit teaches balance. Wisdom refuses extremes that reduce Christianity to either mystical experiences without obedience or hard work without intimacy. **"Let the peace of Christ rule in your hearts" (Colossians 3:15 - AMP)** becomes a daily governor for choices about friendships, media, health, money, and mission.

You will be challenged to trade negativity for hope-filled imagination. Scripture urges us to set our minds on what is true and noble so our future is seeded with promise rather than fear (see Philippians 4:8). You will be invited to replace comparison with calling. God's assignments are tailored, and His pace is kind. Someone else's highlight reel is not your map. Faithfulness in small obediences is still God's path to influence and fruit (see Luke 16:10).

Some pages explore the Bible's supernatural worldview with reverence and care. The aim is never to sensationalize or speculate. The aim is to take scripture seriously, to stay Christ-centered, and to keep ministry grounded in love. Miracles are gifts; wisdom is a command. Healthy disciples pursue both, welcoming God's power while cultivating holy habits—hospitality, integrity, hard work, generosity, and gratitude.

If you are a teenager, a university student, a young professional, or a mentor walking with the next generation, welcome. Expect clear teaching, honest stories, and simple practices you can apply as you go along. Don't just hear, implement. Expect frequent scripture, drawn from translations young readers find accessible, always handled with humility. Expect reminders that grace comes first and performance is never the point. Jesus is the point. Life with Him, in Him, and from Him is the invitation.

Begin with this prayer:

Lord Jesus, You live in me. Teach me to live from Your life. Tune my heart to Your voice. Root me in Your unshakable kingdom. Make my days an offering of love. Amen.

CHAPTER 1

FOUNDATIONS FOR LIVING THE INCARNATE LIFE

I carry a growing concern for our generation when I place it beside the witness of earlier believers. Many saints walked through fire, persecution, and loss, yet carried a love that did not bend. Stories of martyrs from the early centuries through the late medieval period confront my comfort and expose how quickly modern resilience can crack. Pressure comes, and some of us fold. Ease and distraction rarely train a soul for holy endurance. The invitation of the Spirit is not nostalgia for a harsher past. The invitation is the recovery of a life formed by union with Christ that can stand in any age, including ours.

Living the incarnate life means learning to live as men and women indwelt by the risen Christ, embodying His love, wisdom, and power in ordinary places. John writes, **"Love has been perfected among us in this:**

that we may have boldness in the day of judgment; because as He is, so are we in this world." (1 John 4:17 - NKJV). That sentence is not religious poetry. That sentence is a summons to identity. A vessel is named by what it carries. An empty bottle is only a bottle. Fill it with water and it becomes a water bottle. Human beings were created to carry the life of God. Our worth is not set by mirrors, crowds or social media trends. Our worth is set by the One who chooses to dwell within us.

Incarnation as a doctrine celebrates that the eternal Son truly became human without ceasing to be God. Incarnate as a verb points toward embodiment. The church confesses that Jesus Christ is one person in two natures, fully God and fully man. The miracle of salvation is that those who trust Him are joined to Him by the Spirit. Paul compresses the mystery into a single line: "It is no longer I who live, but Christ lives in me." (Galatians 2:20 - NKJV). Union with Christ does not erase our personhood. Union with Christ restores and elevates it by grace. Early teachers expressed this idea in various forms: *the Son became what we are to bring us into fellowship with what He is, not by nature or essence, but through loving participation.*

This reframes discipleship. We were not saved merely to admire Jesus from a distance. We were saved to participate in His life. Jesus, the second Adam, repairs what the first Adam fractured (see Romans 5:12–21). That means the Gospels are not only a record of what God once did in Galilee, but also a record of what God continues to do in Galilee. They are also a revelation of who we are becoming in Him. Jesus says, **"I assure you, the Son can do nothing by Himself; He does only what He sees the Father doing." (John 5:19 - TPT).** Heaven initiates. The Son embodies. The same pattern becomes ours through the Spirit.

Confusion often gathers around the phrase **"in My name."** Scripture does not treat the name of Jesus as a sound to tack onto a sentence. A name in the biblical world speaks of a person, presence, and authority. To act in *His name* is to act from allegiance to His person, alignment with His character, and authorization under His lordship. Language varies across history and culture. Power rests in the Person to whom the name refers. The early church healed and preached **"in the name of Jesus Christ of Nazareth" (Acts 3:6 - NKJV),** which means they stood inside His authority and represented His character. This guards us from magical thinking and calls us to abiding obedience.

Identity precedes activity. Paul tells us to **"let this same attitude and purpose and humble mind be in you which was in Christ Jesus." (Philippians 2:5 - AMP).** He also declares, **"We have the mind of Christ." (1 Corinthians 2:16 - NKJV).** Isaiah's word, **"My thoughts are not your thoughts,"** named the distance of an old covenant estrangement (see Isaiah 55:8–9). The new covenant closes that distance in the Messiah. Believers receive the Spirit who **"searches all things, even the depths of God." (1 Corinthians 2:10 - NASB).** Youth do not need a thinner religion. Youth need thick participation in Christ. The church does not transform the world by slogans. The church becomes a sign of the kingdom when people live as carriers of Jesus' life in kitchens, classrooms, companies, and city streets.

Living the incarnate life does not collapse the Creator–creature distinction. God remains God. We remain human. Grace does not make us divine by nature. Grace unites us to the divine Son so that His life, mind, and mission flow through our humanity. The world sees God's character in the faces, words, and works of those who bear His name.

People form their opinions about God by observing us.

Jesus says, **"Let me give you a new command: Love one another. In the same way I loved you, love one another." (John 13:34 - MSG).** The incarnate life trains a church to love in a way that looks like Jesus.

PRACTICAL APPLICATION

1. **Morning "Christ-in-me" check-in:** Say, *"Jesus, live Your life through me today."* Ask for one person to love like Jesus.

2. **Identity card:** Save this on your lock screen: *"As He is, so are we in this world" (1 John 4:17)*. Read it before school, work, or posting.

3. **"In His Name" filter:** Before a decision, DM or post, ask three checks:

   ✓ **Allegiance** (Am I with Jesus?)
   ✓ **Alignment** (Does this reflect His character?)
   ✓ **Authorization** (Would He sign this?).

4. **Embodiment rep:** Choose one ordinary space (kitchen, classroom, WhatsApp group) and do one Jesus-shaped act of love daily this week.

5. **Scripture immersion:** Read Galatians 2:20 and 1 John 4:17. Write one line that stands out and pray it back to God.

REFLECTION QUESTIONS

1. Where do you tend to "fold" under pressure, and how could union with Christ change that response?

2. What's the difference between using Jesus' name as a formula and acting under His authority?

3. Which ordinary place this week most needs you to embody Jesus' love?

4. How does "identity precedes activity" confront your current to-do list or ambitions?

5. When have you sensed John 5:19—seeing what the Father is doing—and how can you grow in that?

6. What comparison habits (mirrors, crowds, socials) distort your worth, and what will you mute/remove?

ACTIVATION PRAYER

Lord Jesus, thank You that You live in me by Your Spirit. I yield my thoughts, words, and actions to Your life today. Form in me Your mind and teach me to see what the Father is doing. Let Your love shape my responses under pressure so I endure with joy. Train me to act truly **"in Your name"**—in allegiance to Your person, alignment with Your character, and under Your authority. In my ordinary places— kitchen, classroom, conversations—let people meet Your kindness, wisdom, and power through me. I renounce comparison and receive my worth from Your indwelling presence. Live Your life through mine. Make me a faithful carrier of Your heart. In Jesus' name. Amen.

KEY TAKEAWAYS

1. Union with Christ restores identity; **identity precedes activity**.

2. "In His name" means allegiance, alignment, and authorization—not a magic phrase.

3. The Gospels reveal who we're becoming as we participate in Jesus' life.

4. Ordinary places are the primary stage for incarnate living.

5. Endurance grows as Christ's life shapes our responses under pressure.

VERSE FOR MEDITATION

Galatians 2:20 — "I have been crucified with Christ; it is no longer I who live, but Christ lives in me…." (NKJV).

Why it fits: It anchors the chapter's core: you don't perform for God—you participate in Christ's indwelling life.

POST THIS

"Identity before activity—Christ lives in me." #DivineUnion #ChristInMe #YouthEmpowerment #IncarnateLife #WalkItOut

Caption: *"Today I'm choosing participation over performance. Where can I embody Jesus' love—online or in person?"*

CTA: Tag a friend

CHAPTER 2

FROM PRAYER TO MANIFESTATION: PARTICIPATING IN THE FATHER'S WORK

Prayer is not a request tossed toward a silent sky. Prayer is the participation of sons and daughters in the Father's will through the Son by the Spirit. Paul says, **"For no matter how many promises God has made, they are 'Yes' in Christ. And so through Him the 'Amen' is spoken by us to the glory of God"** (2 Corinthians 1:20 - NKJV/NASB sense). Jesus teaches, **"When you pray, believe that you have received it, and it will be yours."** (Mark 11:24 - TPT). Faith is not wishful thinking. Faith is trust in God's character, submission to His wisdom, and obedient steps that fit His revealed will.

Worship often opens our hearts to recognize what the Father is doing. Communities frequently rush from worship into announcements without pausing to agree with God. A better pattern is to let worship lead into scripture-shaped declarations that confess Christ's lordship over our homes, bodies, and neighborhoods. Words are not talismans. Confession aligns us with truth.

"The word is near you, in your mouth and in your heart... that if you confess with your mouth the Lord Jesus and believe in your heart that God has raised Him from the dead, you will be saved." (Romans 10:8–9 - NKJV).

Prophetic encouragement, weighed and tested in community, strengthens and consoles (see 1 Corinthians 14:3, 29). The Spirit moves. The body responds. Heaven's initiative meets earth's obedience.

Genesis offers a paradigm that never grows old. God speaks the world into being (see Genesis 1). Humanity is formed and commissioned to cultivate what God initiates (see Genesis 2). Scripture even notes that certain things had not yet sprouted **"for the Lord God had not caused it to rain on the earth, and there was no man to till the ground."** (Genesis 2:5 - NKJV). Creation flourishes where divine intention and human participation meet. The same pattern extends into redemption. The Spirit empowers and leads. The church acts in love. James refuses any divorce between belief and practice: **"Faith by itself, if it does not have works, is dead." (James 2:17 - NKJV).** The incarnate life is faith with hands, hope with habits, love with labor.

Testimonies of healing, deliverance, provision, and guidance in scripture are not museum artifacts. They are invitations to expectancy under the cross and within the character of Christ. Miracles remain God's works, sovereignly given and wisely timed. **"God also bearing witness both with signs and wonders, with various miracles, and gifts of the Holy Spirit, according to His own will." (Hebrews 2:4 - NKJV).** Paul's life keeps us honest. He knew preservation after stoning and beating (see Acts 14:19–20, 2 Corinthians 11:24–27). He also knew seasons of weakness where grace was sufficient, though the thorn remained (see 2 Corinthians 12:7–10). Expectation without presumption grows mature disciples. A church that prays for the sick should also visit the sick, bring meals, repair roofs, mentor children, and reconcile enemies.

Questions about mortality and immortality deserve careful handling. Scripture teaches that mortality will be swallowed up by life at the resurrection. **"This**

perishable must put on the imperishable, and this mortal must put on immortality." (1 Corinthians 15:53 - NASB). The Spirit gives foretastes now by renewing our mortal bodies for service and perseverance (see Romans 8:11). Saints who met God powerfully did not stop being human. They lived as living sacrifices, which is the shape of Christian worship (see Romans 12:1). Youth can hunger for God's power while staying anchored in the story of the cross and the certain hope of resurrection.

Churches often ask how to move from answered-in-heaven to manifested-on-earth. Scripture gives simple, repeatable paths. Pray according to the will of God revealed in scripture. Agree together. Forgive one another. Act in obedience. Persist with patience. Celebrate small beginnings. Train hands and hearts at home. Households can practice praying for headaches and fevers, declaring Christ's peace over anxiety, blessing children with the Aaronic blessing, and sharing goods with integrity. Formation increases authority. That is why Jesus started His training in living rooms and fishing boats before sending disciples to the nations.

Language matters. Treat **"in Jesus' name"** as more than a closing formula. Live every moment **"in the** name of the Lord Jesus," which means in His presence and under His authority (see Colossians 3:17). Treat worship as more than songs. Worship is submission, adoration, and grateful alignment. Treat prophecy as more than prediction. Prophecy is Christ-centered edification. Treat faith as more than intensity. Faith is fidelity to Jesus. Communities that practice these things become places where heaven's intentions regularly meet earth's realities.

PRACTICAL APPLICATION

Worship → Declaration: After worship, read one promise (for example, 2 Corinthians 1:20, Romans 10:8–10, Colossians 3:17). Declare Christ's lordship over one sphere (school, body, home), then thank God specifically.

Amen Map: Pick one need (anxiety, exams, reconciliation). Find 2–3 matching promises. Under each, write one **Amen step** (obedience you'll take today). For example: Promise—Philippians 4:6–7. Amen step—text a mentor and pray together before study.

Agreement Triad: Form a 2–3 person WhatsApp group. Weekly 10-minute rhythm: share one promise, pray a one-minute agreement, name one action, check in next week.

Household Practice: Pray for simple needs (headaches, favor, peace). Speak the Aaronic blessing nightly (see Numbers 6:24–26). Share goods with integrity (aee Acts 2:45). Track outcomes in a notes app.

"In His Name" AAA Filter: Before a decision/post:

- ✓ **Allegiance** (Am I with Jesus?)
- ✓ **Alignment** (Does this reflect His character?)
- ✓ **Authorization** (Would He sign this?)

If any "no," pause or revise.

Pair Prayer with Mercy: For every prayer request, add one practical act (meal, ride, homework help, roof fix). Prayer + practice = manifestation.

REFLECTION QUESTIONS

1. Where have you treated prayer like wishing instead of partnering, and what would partnership look like this week?

2. Which promise are you claiming without an "Amen step"? What is a clear, small step of obedience?

3. How does seeing "in Jesus' name" as presence/authority change your language and lifestyle?

4. When have you seen worship naturally lead to bold, scripture-shaped declaration? What shifted?

5. How can your home become a training ground for praying, blessing, and serving?

6. Who are two friends you can invite into an agreement rhythm—and what will your first action be?

ACTIVATION PRAYER

Father, thank You that every promise finds its Yes in Jesus. By the Spirit, I add my Amen, not only with my mouth but with obedient steps. Tune my heart in worship to recognize what You are doing, and train my tongue to speak truth that aligns with Your Word. Teach me to live every moment in the name of the Lord

Jesus—in Your presence, under Your authority, for Your glory. Grow in me expectation without presumption: faith that prays for the sick and also serves the suffering. Make my home a place of blessing, agreement, and practice. As I agree with You, give me the courage to forgive, to act, to persist, and to celebrate small beginnings. Let heaven's initiative meet my earthly obedience today. In Jesus' name. Amen.

KEY TAKEAWAYS

1. Prayer is **partnership**: the Father initiates, we add our obedient **Amen**.

2. Worship should flow into **scripture-shaped declarations**, not just announcements.

3. "In Jesus' name" is a lifestyle of presence and authority—not a closing formula.

4. Faith is **fidelity** to Jesus that works through love; belief without action is incomplete.

5. Expect healing and help, while embracing the cross and perseverance.

6. Formation at home increases authority in public; practice in the small, then the big.

VERSE FOR MEDITATION

2 Corinthians 1:20 — "For all the promises of God in Him are Yes, and in Him Amen, to the glory of God through us." (NKJV).

Why it fits: The whole chapter moves from God's **Yes** in Christ to our lived **Amen** on earth.

POST THIS

"Heaven's Yes needs my obedient Amen."
#DivineUnion #ChristInMe #PrayerToPractice
#YouthEmpowerment #WalkItOut #Amen

Caption: *"Today's Amen step:_____
Who's agreeing with me?"*

CTA: Tag two friends to form an Agreement Triad

CHAPTER 3

TRAINING FOR GREATER WORKS: HOME FIRST, THEN THE WORLD

Recent crises revealed fragile systems and unprepared souls. The response God seeks is not panic or spectacle. The response is preparation through basics practiced with devotion. Jesus promises His presence wherever two or three gather in His name (see Matthew 18:20). Families and small groups remain the seedbed of resilient churches. Households can open scripture, pray the Psalms, receive communion with reverence when elders provide, practice confession and forgiveness, and pray for the sick with simple faith. Mastery of the basics is not small. Mastery of basics is foundational.

Jesus promises that those who trust Him will do the works He does, and greater in scope, as His life is lived out through a global body (see John 14:12). The Spirit distributes gifts for the common good and forms fruit that bears the likeness of Jesus (see 1 Corinthians 12:7, Galatians 5:22–23). Christ gives apostles, prophets, evangelists, shepherds, and teachers **"for the equipping of the saints for the work of service, to the building up of the body of Christ... until we all attain to the unity of the faith." (Ephesians 4:11–13 - NASB).** Local congregations should expect all five graces to be present in seed form and should train and release them with humility and order. A church that only hires ministry will remain immature. A church that equips ministry will grow up into Christ.

Incarnate living leans into social repair. Isaiah calls God's people **"repairer of the breach, restorer of streets to dwell in" (Isaiah 58:12 - NKJV).** Jeremiah commands exiles to seek the shalom of their city and pray for it, since their welfare is tied to its welfare (see Jeremiah 29:7). Paul urges believers to **"maintain good works. These things are good and profitable to men." (Titus 3:8 - NKJV).** Youth need a big vision of vocation. Work is worship when it is offered to God for the good of neighbors. The world waits for saints in medicine, research, education, agriculture, the arts, governance, trades, and technology who carry Christ's mind into their craft.

Your practical steps align precisely with scripture, so here they are with greater traction for daily life. First, encourage children and students to pursue callings that bless humanity. Career discernment should ask more than "What pays?" Discernment should ask "What heals?"

"Be fruitful and multiply; fill the earth and subdue it; have dominion" (Genesis 1:28 - NKJV) describes stewardship, not exploitation. Young believers can apprentice themselves to the good of neighbors through study, internships, service projects, and prayerful mentoring.

Second, become participants in the gospel rather than mere messengers. Paul corrects talk-only religion: **"The kingdom of God is not a matter of talk but of power." (1 Corinthians 4:20 - MSG).** Power looks like love expressed through obedience. Share the good news and embody good works. Pray for the sick and sit with the lonely. Confront injustice and practice reconciliation. Teach scripture and tutor children. Preach Christ and pay off a neighbor's debt when the Spirit leads. The gospel advances through holy words welded to holy deeds.

Third, plant something. Creation care is not a trendy add-on. Creation care is part of humanity's first vocation. **"Then the Lord God took the man and put him in the garden of Eden to tend and keep it." (Genesis 2:15 - NKJV).** Plant a tree. Grow herbs. Start a community garden by your church if zoning allows. Teach children to steward soil and water. Small acts train souls to love a world God loves.

Fourth, hold people and places in your heart as a priestly habit. Paul tells the Philippians, **"You have a permanent place in my heart." (Philippians 1:7 - TPT).** Intercession joined to affection softens speech, opens doors, and shifts atmospheres. People change when they are carried in love before God. Systems begin to reform when advocates pray with fidelity and then act with wisdom. Correction without compassion hardens hearts. Love without truth dissolves into sentiment. Priesthood carries both.

Fifth, declare daily your union with Christ. Begin mornings with a simple confession: **"I am in Christ and Christ is in me." (Colossians 1:27 - NKJV).** Let language follow identity. Speak the truth of Galatians 2:20 over your life: **"It is no longer I who live, but Christ lives in me." (NKJV).** This is not a denial of personal responsibility. This is a renunciation of self-reliance so that Christ's life becomes the animating center of your day. Families can practice this together at breakfast or before school runs.

The church cannot remain satisfied with merely counting decisions. Jesus commanded us to make disciples, teaching them to obey everything He commanded, promising to be with us always (see Matthew 28:18–20). A church that lives in union with Christ at home will carry that life into the neighborhood, then the city, and ultimately the nation.

"God can do anything, you know—far more than you could ever imagine or guess or request in your wildest dreams. He does it not by pushing us around but by working within us." (Ephesians 3:20 - MSG).

The glory of God will cover the earth as the waters cover the sea through communities that actually live as His embodied presence for the life of the world.

Preparation is mercy. God is returning us to foundations so that future responsibilities do not crush us. Families are being re-centered. Small circles are being retrained. Gifts are being identified and released. The Spirit is nudging us from talk into participation, from distance into union, from event into formation. Living the incarnate life will send us into schools, labs, farms, studios, clinics, and councils as light that does not flicker. Begin with your family. Extend to your street. Grow toward your city. Walk humbly with your God. The conversation will continue, and the practice will deepen, until the knowledge of the Lord saturates ordinary life.

PRACTICAL APPLICATION

Two-or-Three Rhythm: Read a Gospel paragraph, pray a Psalm, confess/forgive, pray for one need (see Matthew 18:20).

Basics Benchmarks (daily/weekly): Daily 10-minute scripture + prayer; weekly reconciliation check; monthly communion with elder oversight; one hospitality act.

APEST at Home (rotate):

- ✓ *Apostle*—initiate a service project
- ✓ *Prophet*—listen and share scripture encouragement
- ✓ *Evangelist*—invite/serve a neighbor

✓ *Shepherd*—check on someone
✓ *Teacher*—explain one verse

Vocation Lab: Ask "What heals?" Pair one skill/subject with one service act (tutor, fix, mentor, design).

Plant and Steward: Grow one plant or micro-garden; journal what it teaches about care and patience.

Priestly List: Keep five names/places on your heart; pray daily and act when the Spirit nudges.

REFLECTION QUESTIONS

1. Which basic (scripture, prayer, confession, forgiveness, hospitality) is weakest in your home, and what's one change you can make this week?

2. Where do you still "hire ministry" instead of equipping saints, and how can you equip instead?

3. Which grace (apostle, prophet, evangelist, shepherd, teacher) seems most active in you right now, and where will you practice it?

4. How does "work is worship" reshape your view of school/skills/career? Give a concrete example.

5. What breach on your street (relational, physical, spiritual) is God asking you to help repair?

6. How will you hold people/places in your heart without losing truth or courage?

ACTIVATION PRAYER

Jesus, thank You for placing me in a body and in a home where Your life can grow. Train me in the basics until they become reflex: scripture, prayer, communion, confession, forgiveness, and hospitality. By Your Spirit, awaken gifts and form fruit so I serve with love and wisdom. Make my house a seedbed that equips saints, not spectators. Guide my hands in the work that heals, and teach me to carry people and places before You in priestly love. Send me as light that does not flicker—on my street, in my school, and into the city. Root me in union with You so "greater works" flow from daily faithfulness. In Jesus' name. Amen.

KEY TAKEAWAYS

1. **Home is the training ground;** resilient churches grow from resilient households.

2. Jesus' "greater works" scale through a global, equipped body, not isolated heroes.

3. Churches mature by **equipping** every believer, not outsourcing ministry.

4. **Work is worship:** Ask "What heals?" and serve neighbors with skill.

5. Mastery of basics builds authority for public witness.

6. Priestly love holds people/places before God and acts with truth and compassion.

VERSE FOR MEDITATION

Ephesians 4:12–13 — "... for the equipping of the saints for the work of ministry, for the edifying of the body of Christ... till we all come to the unity of the faith and of the knowledge of the Son of God..." (NKJV).

Why it fits: The chapter centers on training that starts at home and matures the whole church.

POST THIS

"Home-trained, world-ready—start with two or three." #DivineUnion #EquipTheSaints #YouthEmpowerment #WorkIsWorship #IncarnateLife

Caption: *"Our two-or-three starts this week. What 'basic' are you practicing first?"*

CTA: Tag two people and set your first 20-minute meetup time.

CHAPTER 4

BECOMING THE VOICE OF GOD

Never be afraid to ask hard questions in the presence of a faithful God. Joy drew me into these conversations at first. Challenge kept me honest. Some pressed me about what I believe. Fun faded for a moment under the weight of scrutiny. Faith steadied me again when I remembered that this is a conversation the church must have. Truth can handle questions. Love can carry tension. The Spirit can form a people who will not break under pressure.

Living in divine union means learning to live as those indwelt by Christ in a way that touches real places with real power. Jesus is the Word made flesh in a once-for-all way that belongs to Him alone (see John 1:14). Believers are not the Incarnation by nature. Believers are the body of Christ by grace, temples of the Holy Spirit, living epistles written by God, and people in whom the Word dwells richly (see 1 Corinthians 12:27, 1 Corinthians 6:19, 2 Corinthians

3:2–3, Colossians 3:16). Paul speaks this mystery plainly: **"It is no longer I who live, but Christ lives in me." (Galatians 2:20 - NKJV).** Jesus calls this daily: deny yourself, take up your cross, and follow (see Luke 9:23). The less our self-rule dominates, the more His life shines through.

Luke 9 sits like a seedbed for this. Jesus gives power and authority to heal and to deliver. He multiplies bread through the hands of the disciples. He demands allegiance above comfort and custom. He reveals His glory on the mountain. He comes down to confront unbelief. He rebukes zeal that wants to torch enemies. He calls for a following that does not look back (see Luke 9). The chapter begins with Jesus sharing His authority and ends with Jesus demanding our obedience. That is how formation works.

Words and presence belong together. Jesus proclaims and heals. He speaks and acts. He embodies the kingdom. Those who belong to Him learn to speak and act as extensions of His life. John writes, **"As He is, so are we in this world." (1 John 4:17 - NKJV).** That sentence stretches our imagination for what a Spirit-filled human life can carry. Identity shapes activity. Vessels are named by what they carry—bottles filled with water become water bottles. Hearts filled with Christ become witnesses to Christ.

"Whatever you do in word or deed, do all in the name of the Lord Jesus" is a way of life, not a magical punctuation mark (see Colossians 3:17). Jesus authorizes disciples to go, to proclaim, to heal, and to drive out darkness. He does not invite spectatorship. He creates participants.

Prayer must be more than requests. Prayer becomes participation. God's Yes in Christ seeks an Amen from a church that believes, confesses, and acts. Faith is not volume or wishfulness. Faith is trust in God's character expressed through obedient steps aligned with God's will. The Amen postures the church to carry out what the Father is doing.

Worship trains this posture. Congregations often sing and then rush to logistics. A wiser rhythm lingers. Declarations rooted in Scripture do not conjure outcomes. Declarations align hearts with reality in Christ. **"The word is near you, in your mouth and in your heart." (Romans 10:8 - NKJV).** The Spirit moves. Sons and daughters respond. The Father initiates. Children participate. Heaven speaks. Earth echoes.

The voice God entrusted to you matters. Proverbs says, **"Death and life are in the power of the tongue." (Proverbs 18:21 - NKJV).** James warns that blessing and cursing should not flow from the same mouth because such springs cannot water gardens well (see James 3:9–12). Scripture joins this to prayer without any sense of contradiction. Bless with your mouth. Intercede with your mouth. Sing with your mouth. Announce the gospel with your mouth. Refuse to partner with slander and backbiting that tear lives apart. Jesus tells us that we will give an account for every careless word (see Matthew 12:36). Speech is not trivial. Speech is stewardship.

Voices shape homes, churches, and histories. Families can be ruined by quiet sarcasm that erodes courage over years. Churches can be healed by steady encouragement that refuses to quit. Cities can be poisoned by fear-mongering that baptizes resentment as prophecy. Nations can be served by truth-telling that bears cost without violence.

Creation groans for the revealing of mature sons and daughters who carry the sound of mercy, justice, and hope (see Romans 8:19–22). Union with Christ gives your voice a new center. The tone of heaven belongs in the mouths of the saints.

PRACTICAL APPLICATION

Voice Audit + Ephesians 4:29 Rule: Track your words (encourage, pray, bless, complain, gossip, sarcasm). Each day, replace one negative with a spoken blessing.

Worship → Declarations: After singing, read one verse (for example, Romans 10:8, Colossians 3:17, Proverbs 18:21) and declare Christ's lordship over your home/school. Add one **Amen step** you'll do today.

Prophetic Encouragement Drill (weekly): Ask the Spirit for a short, scripture-shaped encouragement for someone (see 1 Corinthians 14:3). Write it down, weigh it, and then share it humbly and briefly.

Digital Tongue: Before posting/commenting, use **T.H.I.N.K.** (True, Helpful, Inspiring, Necessary, Kind) + the **AAA filter** (Allegiance, Alignment, Authorization). If any "no," don't post.

Blessing Habit: Speak the Aaronic blessing (see Numbers 6:24–26) over family/friends by name every morning.

Repair with Words + Works: If your words wounded someone, repent directly and pair your apology with a tangible act of service.

REFLECTION QUESTIONS

1. Where do your words most often drift off-mission (home, DMs, jokes, stress), and what practice will redirect them?

2. How does living "in His name" (presence, authority) change your tone online and in person?

3. Which moment this week calls for prophetic encouragement, and how will you weigh it before sharing?

4. When have you seen "words + presence" come together like Jesus—speaking and acting as one?

5. What is one setting where you've partnered with sarcasm or fear-mongering? How will you reverse it?

6. Who needs a blessing from your mouth today, and what verse will shape it?

7. What relationship needs repair because of your speech, and what is your first courageous step?

ACTIVATION PRAYER

Lord Jesus, Word made flesh, steward my mouth for Your glory. Fill me with Your life so my words echo heaven—truthful, kind, courageous, and pure. Teach me to live every moment in Your name—Your presence and authority—so that what I speak aligns with what You are doing. Forgive my careless, cutting, or fearful words, and give me grace to repair what I have damaged. Join my speech with Your presence: proclamation with compassion, declaration with obedience. Make me a living epistle who strengthens hearts, resists slander, and carries hope. Form in me the tone of heaven for my home, church, and city. In Jesus' name. Amen.

KEY TAKEAWAYS

1. **Words are stewardship:** death and life ride on the tongue.

2. **Presence + proclamation:** speak and act together as extensions of Jesus' life.

3. "In Jesus' name" is a **way of life**—allegiance, alignment, authorization.

4. **Prayer → participation:** God's **Yes** seeks our obedient **Amen**.

5. **Voices shape histories:** bless, don't backbite; repair breaches with truth and love.

VERSE FOR MEDITATION

Ephesians 4:29 — "Let no corrupt word proceed out of your mouth, but what is good for necessary edification, that it may impart grace to the hearers." (NKJV).

Why it fits: It captures the chapter's core—your mouth is a ministry that must impart grace.

POST THIS

"Words shape worlds—speak life in Jesus' name."
#DivineUnion #SpeakLife #ChristInMe
#YouthEmpowerment #IncarnateLife #WalkItOut

Caption: *"Today I'm using my voice to bless. Who can I encourage right now?"*

CTA: Tag one person and speak a 1-sentence scripture blessing over them in the comments.

CHAPTER 5

SIGHT AND SOUND: HOW HEAVEN'S INTENTION MEETS EARTH'S REALITY

Genesis teaches a pattern: the Spirit hovers, God speaks, creation responds, and goodness is named (see Genesis 1).

"By faith we understand that the worlds were framed by the word of God." (Hebrews 11:3 - NKJV).

Sight and sound belong to God and are shared with humanity as gifts. God sees in wisdom and speaks in truth. Image-bearers are invited to learn those habits in creaturely ways.

Imagination is not a toy. Imagination is an organ of faith. Paul prays that the **"eyes of your heart may be enlightened." (Ephesians 1:18 - NASB).** Faith sees what God promises before everyone else does. **"Faith** is the assurance of things hoped for, the conviction of things not seen." (Hebrews 11:1 - NASB). Sight without sound stalls. Sound without sight misfires. The church needs hearts that see the Father's intention and mouths that agree with it.

Adam's naming of the animals in Genesis 2 is a case study. God formed beasts and birds and brought them to the man "to see what he would call them; and whatever the man called a living creature, that was its name." (Genesis 2:19 - NASB). Naming does not create essence out of nothing. Naming recognizes identity and confers vocation. The pattern remains instructive. God initiates and forms. Humanity discerns and names. Creation is ordered through a partnership that honors the Creator and dignifies the creature.

Prayer stands in that space. God answers prayer in Christ. Some answers bloom at once in visible ways. Some answers are given as assignments to embody over time. God opened a door for Paul in Troas, yet Paul discerned he could not step through it because his team was not complete (see 2 Corinthians 2:12–13). Heaven's Yes awaited earth's readiness. Jesus did not entrust Himself to certain crowds because He knew what was in man (see John 2:24–25). The Spirit is generous and wise. Manifestation involves timing, formation, and obedience.

Language can be turned toward harm. That warning must sit near our zeal. Elijah's fire on Carmel exposed false gods and called Israel to the Lord. The confrontation was dramatic, and it was followed by renewed rain in a drought-stricken land (see 1 Kings 18). Elijah's next chapter held fear and flight. Jezebel's threat sent him into the wilderness. God met him with food, a gentle voice, and future assignments that included anointing a successor (see 1 Kings 19). The New Testament reads Elijah through Jesus and refuses to baptize violence as zeal. James and John wanted to call down fire when a Samaritan village rejected Jesus; the Lord rebuked them: **"You do not know what kind of spirit you are of; for the Son of Man did not come to destroy men's lives, but to save them." (Luke 9:55–56 - NASB).** The church must learn the difference between prophetic courage and retaliatory fervor. The first loves truth and seeks rescue. The second loves victory and seeks payback.

Eschatology must be handled with hope that honors Jesus. Scripture promises a new heavens and a new earth where righteousness dwells (see 2 Peter 3:13). Revelation sings of a renewed creation where God dwells with His people, wipes tears, and makes all things new (see Revelation 21:1–5). Isaiah imagines long life, healed labor, and reconciled creation (see Isaiah 65:17–25). Paul speaks of the reconciliation of all things in Christ and the restoration spoken of by the prophets (see Colossians 1:19–20, Acts 3:21). Debate lives in the details. Hope stands in the center. The consummation belongs to God. Participation belongs to the church.

Creation care is not a secular hobby. Creation care is a Christian vocation. **"The Lord God took the man and put him in the garden of Eden to tend and keep it." (Genesis 2:15 - NKJV).** Jeremiah counsels exiles to seek the peace of the city and pray for it because their welfare is bound up with the city's welfare (see Jeremiah 29:7). Youth need a vision of vocation that asks what heals, not only what pays. Medicine, research, education, law, trade, agriculture, the arts, technology, and public service become altars where love for God and one's neighbor is offered.

Speech must be stewarded within this hope. The church can baptize doom until doom becomes a habit. The church can also sing mercy until mercy becomes an atmosphere. Jesus refuses the disciples' desire to scorch a town that rejected Him. Jesus teaches His followers to bless those who curse them, to pray for their persecutors, and to overcome evil with good (see Luke 6:27–28, Romans 12:21). The voice of the church must harmonize with the character of her Lord.

Ordinary stories confirm that speech carries weight beyond walls. Slander can make heads ache and hearts heavy without any physical contact. Blessing can lift countenances and heal memories across great distances. **"The smoke of the incense, with the prayers of the saints, ascended before God"** is not poetry aimed at making intercession feel important (Revelation 8:4 - NKJV). Scripture insists that our words rise before God and ripple through creation. Lives can be carried by love before they ever meet our faces. That is holy power. That is holy responsibility.

Bold imagination belongs here. Vision sees what God intends before the crowd believes it is possible. Faith speaks in step with that vision. **"I believed, therefore I spoke"** is the apostolic pattern (2 Corinthians 4:13 - NKJV). The church does not turn faith into technique. The church does not pretend that saying creates reality at will. The church learns to see what the Father is doing and to say what fits the Father's heart. Jesus modeled that dependence perfectly. Disciples learn it progressively.

PRACTICAL APPLICATION

Sight and Sound Warm-Up: Pray, "Lord, enlighten the eyes of my heart" (see Ephesians 1:18). Read one promise. *See* how obedience would look today; then *say* a simple agreement out loud.

Vision Journal: Write one God-shaped picture for your school, home or street (what heals, not just what pays). Add a one-line faith confession that fits scripture.

"Name It" Discernment: For one person or project, ask: *What identity/vocation is God highlighting?* Speak a **blessing-name** that recognizes (not invents) what God is forming (see Genesis 2:19).

Amen Pipeline: For every prayer, note if the answer is a **gift now** or an **assignment over time**. If it's an assignment, list your next two obedience steps and a date to review.

Courage, Not Retaliation: When provoked, pause and ask: **"What spirit am I of?"** (see Luke 9:55–56). Choose rescue-oriented truth over payback rhetoric.

Atmosphere Practice: Replace doom-scroll talk with mercy-speak. Once daily, bless someone *by name* (see Numbers 6:24–26) and send a text of encouragement.

Creation and City Care: Plant something small (a herb or a tree) or pick one neighborhood repair project to act on this month. Journal what it teaches you about God's timing.

REFLECTION QUESTIONS

1. Where is your imagination most formed by fear instead of faith, and how will you retrain it this week?

2. What have you been "naming" in people or projects—does it recognize God's work or your preferences?

3. Which recent prayer is actually an **assignment** waiting on your obedience? What's step one?

4. When did your zeal drift toward retaliation? How would prophetic **rescue** have sounded instead?

5. How do your words shape atmospheres—at home, online, and at church? What habit must change?

6. Where can your vocation (study/skill) practically "repair the breach" right now?

7. How does hope in the new creation (see Revelation 21:1–5) recalibrate your tone and timing today?

ACTIVATION PRAYER

Father, thank You for sharing Your sight and sound with Your children. Enlighten the eyes of my heart to see what You intend, and train my mouth to agree with truth in love. Keep me from techniques that pretend to create; teach me dependence that listens and obeys. Where answers are gifts, help me receive with gratitude; where answers are assignments, give me courage to act with patience and integrity. Form prophetic **courage without retaliation** in me. Let my words bless, my imagination build, and my hands repair what is broken—in people and in places. Anchor me in the hope of a renewed creation, and make my life an echo of Your mercy. In Jesus' name. Amen.

KEY TAKEAWAYS

1. **Imagination is an organ of faith**—we see with the heart before we speak with the mouth.

2. **Naming recognizes identity and vocation;** God initiates, we discern and agree.

3. Some prayers arrive as **gifts**; others as **assignments** that unfold through obedience and timing.

4. **Prophetic courage rescues;** retaliatory fervor seeks payback and misrepresents Jesus.

5. **Speech shapes atmospheres:** sing mercy, not doom; bless and build.

6. **Hope governs tone:** eschatology fuels faithful participation now, not despair.

7. **Creation care is vocation,** not trend—tend and repair what God entrusts.

VERSE FOR MEDITATION

Ephesians 1:18 — "The eyes of your understanding being enlightened; that you may know what is the hope of His calling..." (NKJV).

Why it fits: The chapter centers on seeing with the heart so we can speak and act in step with God's intention.

POST THIS

"See with faith. Speak with love. Obey with hope."
#DivineUnion #EyesOfTheHeart #SpeakLife
#YouthEmpowerment #IncarnateLife #WalkItOut

Caption: *"Today's Amen step:* _____
What are you seeing and saying in faith?"

CTA: Tag one friend and bless them in one sentence in the comments.

CHAPTER 6

FIRE OR MERCY: FRAMING THE FUTURE WITH THE SPIRIT OF JESUS

Voices frame futures. The generation before us handed us worlds built by their words, their prayers, their laws, and their habits. Our voices are building the worlds our children will inhabit. Luke 9 forces a decision between fire and mercy. James and John asked permission to call down fire on the Samaritans who rejected Jesus. A holy shock sits in the Lord's answer: **"You do not know what kind of spirit you are of." (Luke 9:55 - NASB).** The kingdom does not grow by incinerating opponents. The kingdom grows by embodied love, persevering truth, and cruciform power.

Prophetic speech must be distinguished from reactive declaration. Some use scripture to baptize resentment and call it courage. Others use hope to ignore pain and call it faith. Neither rings true to the voice of Jesus.

Prophecy reveals Jesus, builds up the church, and summons repentance that leads to life (see Revelation 19:10, 1 Corinthians 14:3, Acts 11:18). Declarations that harmonize with Christ's character carry weight. Declarations that rebel against His character harm souls. The tongue can set forests ablaze or shade cities with trees planted by wise speech.

Eschatological texts require humility. Believers disagree about timelines and symbols. Scripture remains unanimous about the Lord's return, the final judgment, and the renewal of all things. Fixation on destruction can become a habit that deforms people into cynics. Fixation on triumph can become a habit that deforms people into deniers of suffering. Hopeful realism fits the gospel. The cross and the resurrection teach the tone. Death is faced. Life prevails. Love reigns.

Christ's body has work to do, and that work begins at home. Families can practice worship that lingers long enough to listen. Children can be taught to bless their classmates by name before school. Marriages can confess and forgive after conflict instead of letting resentment harden. Small groups can lay hands on those with headaches and fevers and ask Jesus to heal them. Churches can train the fivefold gifts already present in their people and release them with accountability and joy (see Ephesians 4:11–13). Congregations can adopt classrooms, visit prisons, mentor entrepreneurs, plant gardens, and steward land. Neighborhoods can be strengthened by saints who consistently show up.

Personal formation returns to simple practices that carry power when done in faith. Begin days with confession of union: **"I am in Christ and Christ is in me."** (see Colossians 1:27). Pray Philippians 2:5 in the AMP: **"Let this same attitude and purpose and humble mind be in me which was in Christ Jesus."** Ask the Spirit to open the eyes of your heart to see what the Father is doing (see Ephesians 1:18). Open scripture and let the Word dwell in you richly (see Colossians 3:16). Bring your work into the conversation with God. Ask where mercy is needed. Ask where justice is required. Ask where courage is lacking. Speak life, and then do something that aligns with what you said.

Communal formation follows. Leaders learn to weigh prophetic words rather than weaponize them. Congregations learn to value lament in the same room as rejoicing. Intercessors learn to bless enemies without blessing evil. Evangelists learn to preach grace without excusing sin. Teachers learn to handle texts that terrify with tenderness and truth. Apostles learn to build without despising small beginnings. Shepherds learn to guard without smothering. Formation creates capacity for holy speech.

Some in our circle asked helpful and challenging questions. One asked whether talk of manifesting reality risks legitimizing evil. The concern is valid. The human capacity to shape outcomes through speech can be turned toward harm. Scripture answers by commanding our tongues into the service of love. **"Let no corrupt word proceed out of your mouth, but what is good for necessary edification." (Ephesians 4:29 - NKJV).** Another pressed the meaning of Jesus' promise about preparing a place. Union reframes that promise in present tense as well as future hope. **"He raised us up with Him, and seated us with Him in the heavenly places in Christ Jesus." (Ephesians 2:6 - NASB).** The Lord will come again. The Lord is with us now. The church already shares His life even as she waits for His appearing.

Hope grows when we refuse escapism. If salvation were only about departure, saints would disappear on the day of conversion. God keeps us here on purpose. **"We are His workmanship, created in Christ Jesus** for good works, which God prepared beforehand so that we would walk in them." (Ephesians 2:10 - NASB). You are here because you have a purpose. The Spirit trains a people to infiltrate darkness with light, to answer despair with presence, to confront lies with truth, and to counter hate with patient love. Creation will not be healed by spectators. Creation will be healed by sons and daughters who carry the life of the Son into every sphere. Are you a son or daughter?

This is why you must become conscious of the voice you have become on the earth. Your words are not throwaway breath. Your prayers are not background noise. Your declarations are not decorations for worship sets. Your speech is priestly. Your voice is entrusted. Use it to bless and not to curse. Use it to frame futures that look like the Father's heart. Use it to lift neighbors into hope. Use it to name people with dignity instead of labels. Use it to bring the tone of heaven into rooms that forgot what kindness sounds like.

The future does not belong to cynicism. The future belongs to the Lamb. "God can do anything, you know—far more than you could ever imagine or guess or request in your wildest dreams... by working within us, His Spirit deeply and gently within us." **(Ephesians 3:20 - MSG).** Live as those in whom He works. Speak as those through whom He loves. Act as those by whom He blesses. The knowledge of the Lord will cover the earth as the waters cover the sea through people who carry Christ's voice into every valley and every street.

PRACTICAL APPLICATION

Fire→Mercy Pause: When provoked, breathe, ask: *"What spirit am I of?"* (see Luke 9:55). Rewrite your response to rescue, not retaliate.

Priestly Mouth Habit: Each morning, speak Ephesians 4:29 over your day; each night, bless three people by name (see Romans 12:14, Numbers 6:24–26).

Weigh-Before-You-Say: For any "prophetic" impression: write it, test it with scripture and the character of Jesus, and (if possible) run it by 1–2 mature believers (see 1 Corinthians 14:29). Share humbly, briefly, and with accountability.

Home Liturgy of Listening: Linger after worship to listen; confess, forgive; pray for small needs (headaches, anxieties); commission one simple act of mercy for the week.

Mercy + Works Pairing: For every strong opinion you speak online, pair one tangible act of love offline (meal, ride, homework help, apology).

Hope Tone Check: Replace doom-talk with a hope sentence from Revelation 21:1–5 or Ephesians 3:20; keep it as your day's caption/lock-screen.

Neighborhood Blessing Walk (weekly): Walk your street and speak peace over homes, schools, and shops; greet people kindly (see Jeremiah 29:7).

REFLECTION QUESTIONS

1. Where do your words most easily slip from prophetic courage into retaliatory heat? What would rescue-oriented truth sound like instead?

2. Which recent "word" or opinion did you share without weighing? How will you repair or clarify it?

3. How can your home practice (listening, blessing, forgiving) reshape your public tone?

4. What small, consistent act of mercy can you pair with your strongest online topic?

5. In what ways has end-times talk shaped you toward cynicism or denial? How will hope recalibrate your voice?

6. Who needs you to name them with dignity this week, and what scripture will shape that blessing?

7. What would it look like for your local church to release fivefold gifts with joy **and** accountability?

ACTIVATION PRAYER

Lord Jesus, You did not come to destroy lives but to save them. Conform my spirit to Yours. Steward my mouth so my words bless, build, and bring people toward Your heart. Teach me to weigh what I think I hear, to speak only what aligns with Your character, and to pair every declaration with obedient love. Cleanse reactive speech from me. Fill my home with listening, confession, forgiveness, and healing prayer. Make my church a place where gifts are released with tenderness and truth. Anchor my hope in Your return and Your present work within us. Use my voice to frame futures that look like Your mercy. In Jesus' name. Amen.

KEY TAKEAWAYS

1. **Your voice frames futures;** speech is priestly stewardship, not throwaway breath.

2. Jesus rejects retaliatory zeal; **mercy is the tone** of the kingdom (see Luke 9:55–56).

3. **Prophecy reveals Jesus,** builds the church, and summons repentance, not payback.

4. **Hopeful realism** holds cross and resurrection together—facing pain while expecting life.

5. Formation starts at home; **linger, listen, bless, forgive, heal,** then serve your city.

6. Pair strong words with **strong works** of love.

VERSE FOR MEDITATION

Luke 9:55–56 — "But He turned and rebuked them... 'For the Son of Man did not come to destroy men's lives but to save them.'" (NKJV).

Why it fits: It sets the chapter's plumb line—mercy over fire as the Spirit of Jesus.

POST THIS

"Choose mercy over fire—your voice frames futures."
#DivineUnion #SpeakMercy #ChristInMe
#YouthEmpowerment #IncarnateLife #WalkItOut

Caption: *"Today I'm speaking life here. My mercy-action: _____."*

CTA: Tag one friend and bless them in one sentence in the comments.

CHAPTER 7

RENEWING THE MIND: THE DOORWAY TO TRANSFORMATION

A new year always sneaks up on us with a gentle insistence. The calendar turns, and our stories keep unfolding. God's goodness meets us again, which means hope still has room to work. Possibility remains open. The world can still be changed by people who say yes to Christ's life within them. Romans 12 stands like a doorway into that life. **"Present your bodies a living and holy sacrifice, acceptable to God, which is your spiritual service of worship... be transformed by the renewing of your mind." (Romans 12:1–2 - NASB).** Paul puts worship and thought in the same breath. Bodies offered. Minds renewed. Lives transformed.

Transformation does not begin with better outcomes. Transformation begins with a different mind. The word Paul uses for "transformed" carries the sense of being changed from the inside out. The Spirit does this work, yet the mind participates. **"Let this same attitude and purpose and humble mind be in you which was in Christ Jesus." (Philippians 2:5 - AMP).** The goal is not a mind emptied of thought but a mind filled with Christ's perspective. The mind can be closed by fear, pride, or familiarity. The mind can be opened by faith, humility, and love. Closed minds calcify around yesterday's light. Renewed minds stay tender toward the God who still speaks through scripture and by His Spirit.

Openness is not gullibility. Openness is teachability. Scripture remains the anchor. **"All Scripture is given by inspiration of God and is profitable for doctrine, for reproof, for correction, for instruction in righteousness." (2 Timothy 3:16 - NKJV).** The Spirit remains the teacher. **"The Helper, the Holy Spirit... will teach you all things and bring to your remembrance all that I said to you." (John 14:26 - NASB).** The church remains the testing ground. **"Test everything; hold fast what is good." (1 Thessalonians 5:21 - ESV/NKJV sense).** A renewed mind stands under the Word, listens to the Spirit, and walks with the saints.

A renewed mind changes how we read reality. The world trains us to be conformed to patterns of rivalry, fear, and self-protection. The kingdom renews us to love, courage, and self-giving. Paul says this renewed mind "proves" or "discerns" the will of God—what is good, acceptable, and perfect (see Romans 12:2). Discernment is not guesswork for experts. Discernment is the birthright of people saturated in the Word and yielded to the Spirit. The promise stretches further still: **"We have the mind of Christ." (1 Corinthians 2:16 - NKJV).** That sentence is not a boast. That sentence is a stewardship.

Union with Christ frames everything that follows. Believers are not the Incarnation by nature; only Jesus is the Word made flesh in that once-for-all sense (see John 1:14). Believers are His body by grace, temples of the Holy Spirit, living letters written by God (see 1 Corinthians 12:27, 1 Corinthians 6:19, 2 Corinthians 3:2–3). Life in Christ moves beyond admiration into participation. Minds renewed in Christ begin to think with His heart about enemies and neighbors, money and time, bodies and work, worship and witness. **"As He is, so are we in this world." (1 John 4:17 - NKJV).** That is identity before it becomes activity.

The invitation asks for courage. Some fear an open mind because openness has been confused with compromise. Paul calls for something older and sturdier: humility before the God who is not finished revealing His wisdom through scripture and by the Spirit. Isaiah heard the Lord say, **"Behold, I will do a new thing; now it shall spring forth, shall you not know it?" (Isaiah 43:19 - NKJV).** New does not cancel the old; new fulfills the promise buried in the old. A renewed mind learns to recognize fulfillment when it arrives.

Youth need this renewal. Students carry questions that modern slogans cannot answer. The renewed mind can hold mystery without abandoning truth, stretch toward more without despising foundations, and welcome the Spirit's leading without sidelining the Word. **"If any of you lacks wisdom, let him ask of God, who gives to all liberally." (James 1:5 - NKJV).** The Father is not stingy with understanding. The Son shares His mind. The Spirit searches the depths of God and makes them known to us (see 1 Corinthians 2:10). This is the doorway. Walk through it.

PRACTICAL APPLICATION

Morning Romans 12 Reset: Present your body to God (see Romans 12:1), then pray: *"Lord, renew my mind today."* Read one verse and turn it into a one-sentence confession.

R.E.N.E.W. Loop (use all week): Recognize the thought → Examine by scripture → Name God's truth → Exchange old thought with a spoken confession → Walk it out with one concrete action.

Teachability Practice: Ask the Spirit, "What are You showing me in Your Word?" (see John 14:26). Share one takeaway with a mentor/friend and invite feedback (see 1 Thessalonians 5:21).

Wisdom on One Decision: Bring one real choice (friendship, money, time, media) to God (see James 1:5). Write what scripture says, what wise counsel adds, and your next faithful step.

Feed > Fast: Replace 30 minutes of scrolling with 10 minutes Word (see 2 Timothy 3:16), 10 minutes prayer, 10 minutes silence/journaling. Track what changes in your mood and choices.

Identity→Activity Check: Before posting, spending, responding, ask: *"As He is, so am I in this moment?"* (see 1 John 4:17). If not, adjust your action to match your identity.

REFLECTION QUESTIONS

1. Where do you notice "this-age" patterns (rivalry, fear, self-protection) shaping your reactions?

2. What would "the mind of Christ" (see Philippians 2:5) look like in one tense relationship you're in?

3. When have you confused openness with compromise? How can you practice **teachability** with strong anchors?

4. Which scripture most directly corrects your recurring unhelpful thought—and how will you confess it daily?

5. Whose voice forms your thinking most (God's Word, socials, friends, fears)? What rebalancing is needed?

6. What decision needs wisdom right now, and what would a small, faithful step today be?

7. How will you test new insights with scripture, the Spirit's peace, and the church's counsel?

ACTIVATION PRAYER

Father, I present my body as a living sacrifice. By Your Spirit, renew my mind. Let the attitude of Jesus fill my thoughts—humble, obedient, and courageous. Train me to recognize lies, anchor in Your Word, and exchange old patterns for Christ-shaped truth. Give me wisdom for today's decisions and teach me to test everything, holding fast to what is good. Make my imagination an organ of faith that sees what You intend, and my mouth a servant of truth spoken in love. As I abide in Christ, transform me from the inside out so my life proves Your good, acceptable, and perfect will. In Jesus' name. Amen.

KEY TAKEAWAYS

1. Transformation starts **in the mind** and shows up in the life (see Romans 12:1–2).

2. **Teachability ≠ gullibility**—stay anchored in scripture, taught by the Spirit, and tested in community.

3. **Identity precedes activity**—think with Christ before acting (see 1 John 4:17, Philippians 2:5).

4. Discernment is a **birthright** of Word-saturated, Spirit-led believers (see 1 Corinthians 2:16).

5. Humility recognizes God's "new" as fulfillment, not fad (see Isaiah 43:19).

6. Youth can hold **mystery without abandoning truth** when the mind is renewed.

VERSE FOR MEDITATION

Romans 12:2 — "And do not be conformed to this world, but be transformed by the renewing of your mind..." (NKJV).

Why it fits: It names the doorway—mind renewal that proves God's will in daily life.

POST THIS

"Renew your mind. Reframe your world."
#DivineUnion #MindOfChrist #YouthEmpowerment
#IncarnateLife #Romans12 #WalkItOut

Caption: *"Today's R.E.N.E.W. swap:* _____
→ _____."

CTA: Tag a friend and share the verse you're confessing this week.

CHAPTER 8

SCRIPTURE, SPIRIT, AND THE COURAGE TO LEARN

Every disciple inherits teachers, traditions, and treasured phrases. These can either serve to promote growth or stunt it. Doctrine matters because ideas shape lives. Doctrine, however, is not God. Doctrine is our best articulation of what scripture teaches. Scripture names several kinds of doctrine, including "doctrines of men" and "doctrines of demons" to be rejected (see Matthew 15:9, 1 Timothy 4:1). Scripture also celebrates sound teaching and even speaks of adorning "the doctrine of God our Savior" by our lives (see Titus 2:10). The point is simple: teaching must be tested and refined as the church keeps listening to scripture under the tutelage of the Spirit.

A renewed mind refuses two shortcuts. The first shortcut treats tradition as untouchable. The second shortcut treats novelty as unquestionable. Jesus confronted traditions that nullified God's Word while He fulfilled the scriptures the traditions misread (see Mark 7:13, Luke 24:27). The Bereans modeled a faithful posture: they received new teaching "with all readiness" and examined the scriptures daily to see whether these things were so (see Acts 17:11)— readiness without examination drifts. Examination without readiness calcifies. Renewal holds both.

The Spirit's role deserves special clarity. Jesus promised the Spirit would guide us into all truth and glorify the Son (see John 16:13–14). The Spirit never contradicts scripture; the Spirit illumines scripture and applies it to hearts, homes, and histories. The Spirit searches the depths of God and makes known what we need for obedience now (see 1 Corinthians 2:10–12). This is why teachability matters. Pride cannot learn. Fear cannot listen. Love learns and listens. **"Let the word of Christ dwell in you richly"** is a command aimed at communities who sing, correct, forgive, and pray together until scripture lives in them (see Colossians 3:16 - NKJV).

Questions about mystical experiences belong inside this frame, not outside it. Scripture itself witnesses to visions, dreams, and encounters. Scripture also warns against counterfeit spiritualities that promise power without repentance, shortcuts without the cross, spectacle without love. The renewed mind does not despise spiritual gifts; the renewed mind pursues love and earnestly desires spiritual gifts, especially those that build up others (see 1 Corinthians 14:1–3). Gifts are not badges. Gifts are tools for service. Love remains the measure.

Claims that "we cannot know God" need careful nuance. Believers cannot know God exhaustively. Believers can know God truly. Jesus prayed, **"This is eternal life, that they may know You, the only true God, and Jesus Christ whom You have sent." (John 17:3 - NASB).** Paul's longing **"that I may know Him"** rose from decades of encounter and obedience, not ignorance (see Philippians 3:10). Knowing God is relational participation that deepens through a lifetime. New light does not despise old light. New light often sends us back to the same passages with eyes that notice glory we missed.

Fear of people often shadows this journey—a learner who asks questions risks misunderstanding and exclusion. The renewed mind must choose obedience over image. Peter, James, and John saw the glory of God on a mountain and wanted to camp there. Jesus led them back down into a crowd that needed healing and a cross that would save the world (see Luke 9:28–43). Formation is not escape. Formation is readiness to serve. The Spirit's classroom includes kitchens, clinics, classrooms, construction sites, and council meetings. Disciples learn with Bibles open and sleeves rolled.

PRACTICAL APPLICATION

BEREAN-15: *Read* a passage → *Receive* with readiness → *Examine* with cross-references → *Apply* one step → *Note* one question (see Acts 17:11).

T.E.S.T. any teaching: Text—in context; Echo—whole counsel of scripture + historic core; Spirit—does it glorify Jesus and grow love/holiness? (see John 16:13–14, Galatians 5:22–23) Team—submit it to trusted leaders/community (see 1 Thessalonians 5:21).

Two-Guardrail Drill: Ask of every idea: *Am I treating tradition as untouchable? Am I treating novelty as unquestionable?* Adjust toward humble renewal.

Word-Dwell Practice: Let Colossians 3:16 shape a small group: sing a verse, share a correction, pray one promise, and forgive one offense.

Gifts-with-Love Rep: Pursue love first (see 1 Corinthians 14:1). Share one short, scripture-shaped encouragement this week; keep it Christ-exalting and edifying.

Courage to Learn Move: Bring one hard question to a mentor. Arrive with verses, listen without defensiveness, and leave with one action.

REFLECTION QUESTIONS

1. Where do you default to "untouchable tradition" or "unquestionable novelty," and why?

2. When you T.E.S.T. a recent teaching, which part (Text/Echo/Spirit/Team) needs more attention from you?

3. How can you let the Word *dwell richly* in your friendships or small group this week?

4. What spiritual gift can you practice that will most build up someone else right now?

5. Where has fear of people silenced your learning—what courageous step will you take?

6. What's one mystical/experiential moment you should write down and test by scripture and fruit?

7. How does "know truly, not exhaustively" reshape your expectations about knowing God?

ACTIVATION PRAYER

Spirit of Truth, thank You for guiding the church into all truth and glorifying Jesus. Make me teachable— ready to receive and diligent to examine. Anchor me in Your Word, and guard me from pride that cannot learn or fear that will not listen. Let the Word of Christ dwell richly in me and among my community. Purify my motives so every gift I practice exalts Jesus and edifies others. Please give me the courage to ask hard questions, patience to test what I hear, and humility to be corrected. Form in me a mind renewed by scripture and led by the Spirit, so my life adorns the doctrine of God our Savior. In Jesus' name. Amen.

KEY TAKEAWAYS

1. Doctrine must be **tested and refined** by scripture, in the Spirit, within community.

2. Avoid two shortcuts: **untouchable tradition** and **unquestionable novelty**.

3. The Spirit never contradicts scripture; He **illumines and applies** it to obedient lives.

4. **Readiness + Examination** (Berean posture) keeps hearts soft and minds sharp.

5. Spiritual gifts are **tools for service**, measured by love and fruit, not spectacle.

6. We know God **truly (not exhaustively)** through lifelong, relational participation.

VERSE FOR MEDITATION

Acts 17:11 — "...they received the word with all readiness, and searched the Scriptures daily to find out whether these things were so." (NKJV).

Why it fits: It nails the chapter's posture—open hearts and examining minds.

POST THIS

"Open Bible. Open heart. Learn bravely."
#DivineUnion #BereanPosture #SpiritAndScripture
#YouthEmpowerment #IncarnateLife #WalkItOut

Caption: *"Today's T.E.S.T.: _____.
What are you examining with the Word?"*

CTA: Tag a friend you trust to test new ideas with you
this week.

CHAPTER 9

LIVING INSIDE GOD'S PRESENCE: FROM INSIGHT TO IMITATION

Paul's words to the Athenians still steady the soul: **"In Him we live and move and have our being."** (Acts 17:28 - NKJV). God is not distant. God is present to His creation and perfectly aware of our days. The Son took flesh, suffered, died, rose, and reigns. The Spirit indwells those who trust Jesus. Union with Christ does not mean God becomes us or we become God by nature. Union means the triune God shares His life with us so that we participate in His love, holiness, and mission. **"Christ in you, the hope of glory"** names this miracle (see Colossians 1:27 - NKJV).

Renewed minds learn to walk this miracle into ordinary hours. Bodies become instruments of righteousness at work, at play, and at rest (see Romans 6:13). Tongues become holy, speaking life instead of curse, blessing enemies instead of nursing grievances (see Romans 12:14, Proverbs 18:21). Imaginations become sanctified, seeing neighbors in the light of the cross and seeing possibilities through the lens of the resurrection. Faith confesses with honesty, *"I cannot change a heart,"* then acts with courage, *"I can love faithfully while the Spirit works."*

Romans 12 shows the fruit of renewed minds. Gifts become service. Prophecy accords with faith. Generosity looks cheerful. Leadership looks diligent. Mercy looks warm. Hospitality opens the door. Hope rejoices. Tribulation is endured. Prayer remains devoted. Peace is pursued. Evil is overcome with good (see Romans 12:3–21). None of this is possible on human strength alone. All of this becomes plausible when hearts are yielded, minds are renewed, and bodies are offered.

Conversations about "energy," "frequency," and "vibration" can be translated into Christian speech without embarrassment or superstition. Scripture already gives a vocabulary for reality shaped by voice and presence. God speaks and worlds are framed (see Hebrews 11:3). Blessing and cursing carry real effects (see James 3:9–10). Worship enthrones God's rule among His people (see Psalm 22:3). Prophetic encouragement strengthens, exhorts, and comforts (see 1 Corinthians 14:3). The church does not treat words as magic. The church treats words as stewardship—renewed minds steward speech to align with the Father's heart and the Son's way.

Claims that God "experiences" our lives through us must also be held carefully. The Lord Jesus is a merciful High Priest who sympathizes with our weaknesses and was tempted in every respect yet without sin (see Hebrews 4:15). God knows us perfectly, carries us faithfully, and indwells us truly, yet He remains holy, separate from sin's stain. This distinction preserves worship and fuels hope. The Holy One draws near to transform, not to be tainted. Holiness is not fragility. Holiness is fullness that heals.

The road forward will ask for courage and patience. Minds formed by rivalry do not become Christlike overnight. The Spirit is a master teacher who loves process. The metaphor remains the same across centuries: babies grow into children, then into adolescents, and finally into adults. Doctrinal primers serve like alphabet books. Deeper study serves like literature and science. Life with God is not graduation from learning. Life with God is a deeper learning in love. **"His mercies... are new every morning."**

(Lamentations 3:22–23 - NKJV). New mercies do not erase yesterday's grace; new mercies add to it.

One practical warning deserves a final word. Revelation 3 pictures Jesus knocking on a door and promising fellowship to those who open (see Revelation 3:20). The image speaks to believers who drifted into lukewarm comfort. The door we open is not a portal into doctrines detached from life. The door is a heart. The dinner is communion with Christ. The result is renewed zeal, restored love, and a church that hears what the Spirit says. Keep the door unlatched. Keep the table set. Keep the mind soft to scripture and the will soft to obedience.

PRACTICAL APPLICATION

Presence Pauses: Breathe and say, *"In You I live and move and have my being"* (see Acts 17:28). Add: *"Christ in me, I in Christ"* (see Colossians 1:27).

Offer Your Body (see Romans 6:13): Choose one concrete act today that makes your body an instrument of righteousness—serve, work with integrity, rest without guilt, or show up on time for someone.

Sanctify the Tongue: Before you speak or post, run Ephesians 4:29: *Will this impart grace?* Replace complaints with a spoken blessing over a person or place.

Redeem Imagination: Pick one person or situation and view it through the cross and resurrection. Write two "resurrection possibilities," then take one small step toward it.

Romans 12 Lab (one trait per day): Mercy (warm response), Generosity (cheerful gift), Leadership (diligent task), Hospitality (open your table/DM), Hope (rejoice), Perseverance (endure), Prayer (devote).

Keep the Door Unlatched (see Revelation 3:20): Schedule a daily "table moment" (5–10 min). Invite Jesus, give thanks, listen in silence, then obey one nudge.

Bless Your 'Hard Person': Pray Romans 12:14 by name and do one quiet kindness this week.

REFLECTION QUESTIONS

1. When today do you most forget God's nearness, and what cue will bring you back to awareness?

2. Which part of your body (eyes, hands, tongue, feet) needs fresh consecration to righteousness?

3. How can you translate "energy/frequency" talk into scripture-shaped practices without superstition?

4. Which Romans 12 trait is weakest in you right now, and what is one micro-action to grow it today?

5. What would speaking *life* to an enemy sound like this week?

6. Where are you impatient with your growth— what faithful, child-to-adult step is next?

7. How will you keep your daily "table moment" open so insight becomes imitation?

ACTIVATION PRAYER

Father, thank You that in You I live and move and have my being. Lord Jesus, dwell richly in me—make my body an instrument of righteousness, my mind a place of Your peace, and my tongue a servant of grace. Holy Spirit, keep me aware of Your presence in ordinary hours. Train my imagination to see through the cross and resurrection, and my actions to match what I confess. Grow in me the Romans 12 life—cheerful generosity, diligent leadership, warm mercy, steady prayer, and courageous hospitality. Guard me from empty talk and magical thinking; teach me to steward words as worship and service. I open the door to You—come in, shape my desires, and send me in love. In Jesus' name. Amen.

KEY TAKEAWAYS

1. **Presence is the context of life:** we live *in* God; Christ lives *in* us.

2. **Insight must become imitation:** bodies offered, minds renewed, tongues sanctified.

3. **Speech is stewardship, not magic;** bless and build in step with Christ's character.

4. **Romans 12 is a weekly workout** that turns gifts into service and love into action.

5. **Translate cultural language** ("energy or frequency") into scripture-shaped practices centered on Jesus.

6. **Growth is patient and hopeful;** keep the door open to daily communion and obedience.

VERSE FOR MEDITATION

Acts 17:28 — "For in Him we live and move and have our being." (NKJV).

Why it fits: It anchors the chapter's theme—constant awareness of God's nearness, shaping words, work, and witness.

POST THIS

"Practice His presence: think Christ, speak life, love boldly."
#DivineUnion #PracticeHisPresence #ChristInMe
#YouthEmpowerment #IncarnateLife #WalkItOut

Caption: *"Today's presence cue: _____.*
My Romans 12 action: _____."

CTA: Tag one friend you'll bless by name today and write a one-sentence blessing in the comments.

CHAPTER 10

ROMANS 8 AND THE SOUND OF SONS

Welcome to the opening of a door. Hope still has room to work. Romans 8 gives us language for that hope. **"There is therefore now no condemnation for those who are in Christ Jesus."** The Spirit sets us free from the law of sin and death, teaches us to set our minds on life and peace, and bears witness with our spirit that we are God's children. Creation itself is "groaning," waiting for the revealing of the sons and daughters of God. The Spirit also "groans," interceding for us with wordless depths (see Romans 8:1–27). Paul stacks the vocabulary of sound—groanings, intercession, witness—beside the vocabulary of mind and sonship. It is as if he is saying that redeemed thinking has a sound, and redeemed belonging has a resonance that the world can feel.

Discussion of frequency, vibration, and sound is often relegated to studios and science labs, but scripture is not reticent about sound. God's voice thunders and splinters cedars; the heavens declare God's glory; the Spirit comes with a sound like a rushing wind; prisons shake at midnight praise (see Psalm 29, Psalm 19, Acts 2, Acts 16). When the Bible uses "groan," it names a sound deeper than sentences—the ache of the world and the ache of God's people for glory. Your life in Christ has that sound. Your worship has more going on than syllables. Your obedience carries a resonance that travels beyond your hearing.

Each believer carries a unique "voiceprint." No two testimonies are the same, no two gifts harmonize in exactly the same register, and yet in the Spirit we come "with one accord" (see Acts 2:1). Accord is not uniformity of words; it is unity of heart, purpose, and praise. Think orchestra rather than unison chant—many timbres, one song. This is why the New Testament pictures the church as a body with many members, each **"according to the grace given"** (see Romans 12). In Christ, diversity becomes harmony, and harmony becomes power.

Here is a guardrail worth naming out loud. Only Jesus is the Word made flesh in the once-for-all sense (see

John 1:14). By grace, however, we are His body, His temple, His workmanship, indwelt by His Spirit (see 1 Corinthians 12:27; 6:19, Ephesians 2:10). So when we speak about a "sound" coming from our lives, we are not flirting with magic or making sound a mechanism that forces God's hand. We are naming a biblical pattern: God speaks and creates; God sings over His people; God's people bless and curse with their tongues; praise enthrones God's rule among His people; prophetic encouragement strengthens, exhorts, and comforts (see Genesis 1, Zephaniah 3:17, Proverbs 18:21, Psalm 22:3, 1 Corinthians 14:3). Do you see the divine pattern? Words are not tricks. Words are stewardships. Love is the measure. Jesus is the plumb line.

If creation is groaning for the reveal of mature sons and daughters, then part of our maturity is learning to steward our sound—our speech, our singing, our silence, our intercession—so it agrees with the Father's heart. The Spirit's "wordless" intercession teaches us that some of the deepest work God does in and through us moves beneath vocabulary. Tears can pray. A holy hush can preach. A shared "Amen" can turn a room. Faith has a resonance.

PRACTICAL APPLICATION

No-Condemnation Reset: When shame or self-accusation hits, speak Romans 8:1 aloud. Confess any real sin, receive forgiveness (see 1 John 1:9), and take one small obedience step that fits grace.

Mind on Life and Peace: Set a timer for 3 minutes. Breathe in: *"Spirit of life"* (see Romans 8:2). Breathe out: *"Set my mind on life and peace"* (see Romans 8:6). Name one anxious thought and exchange it for a Romans 8 promise.

Abba Breath Prayer: Inhale *"Abba."* Exhale *"I belong."* Repeat 7 times. Let the Spirit bear witness with your spirit (see Romans 8:15–16).

Resonance Audit: Track your "sound" for one day: blessing, intercession, worship, silence, complaint. Replace one complaint with a spoken blessing (see Proverbs 18:21, Romans 12:14).

Groan to God: Practice wordless intercession for two people and one place. Let sighs and tears become prayer (see Romans 8:26–27). Finish with a simple "Amen."

One-Accord Circle: With 2–3 friends: read one Romans 8 verse, each shares a one-sentence encouragement, sing/pray briefly *"with one accord"* (see Acts 2:1), and agree on one act of love.

Midnight Praise: If you wake anxious or feel pressed, offer a short praise before sleep (or right then). Let praise shake the prison of fear (see Acts 16:25–26).

REFLECTION QUESTIONS

1. Where does condemnation still narrate your self-talk, and what Romans 8 truth will replace it?

2. What does your life "sound" like at home or online—blessing, intercession, complaint, or silence?

3. When have you felt the Spirit's witness of sonship, and how can you cultivate that awareness daily?

4. What would a "one accord" expression look like in your small group this month?

5. Where can your obedience carry a resonance beyond words—quiet service, steady kindness, faithful presence?

6. Which Romans 8 promise are you stewarding poorly—and what concrete step will honor it?

7. How can your unique "voiceprint" harmonize with others instead of competing with them?

ACTIVATION PRAYER

Father, thank You that there is now no condemnation in Christ Jesus. Holy Spirit, set my mind on life and peace, and bear witness with my spirit that I am Your child. Teach me the sound of sonship—truth without shame, worship without show, intercession that reaches deeper than words. Align my speech, my singing, my silence, and my actions with the heart of Jesus. Let my life carry a resonance that blesses homes, heals memories, and strengthens the church. Make me quick to say "Amen" to Your will and courageous to walk it out. May creation hear hope through my obedience today. In Jesus' name. Amen.

KEY TAKEAWAYS

1. **No condemnation** is the starting note of sonship (see Romans 8:1).

2. The Spirit frees, **resets the mind**, and **bears witness** that we belong to God (see Romans 8:2, 6, 16).

3. Creation **groans** and the Spirit **groans**—our lives add a hopeful "Amen" (see Romans 8:22–27).

4. Your "sound" is stewarded through speech, singing, silence, and intercession—**not magic; stewardship.**

5. Harmony > uniformity: many "voiceprints," one accord, greater power (see Romans 12, Acts 2:1).

6. Obedience gives worship a resonance that travels beyond words.

VERSE FOR MEDITATION

Romans 8:16 — "The Spirit Himself bears witness with our spirit that we are children of God." (NKJV).

Why it fits: It captures the chapter's heart—sonship has a sound the Spirit Himself confirms.

POST THIS

"No condemnation—carry the sound of sonship." #DivineUnion #SoundOfSons #NoCondemnation #ChristInMe #YouthEmpowerment #WalkItOut

Caption: *"Today my Romans 8 promise: _____. My one-accord action: _____."*

CTA: Tag two friends to join a 15-minute One-Accord Circle this week.

CHAPTER 11

THE BROODING SPIRIT AND THE BIRTH OF NEW WORLDS

"The earth was without form, and void; and darkness was on the face of the deep. And the Spirit of God was hovering over the face of the waters." (Genesis 1:2 - NKJV).

Before a single creature was named, before light was called good, scripture shows us the Spirit brooding—hovering like a mother bird over unformed depths. Then God speaks. Worlds answer. John 6:63 helps us hear Genesis properly: **"The words that I have spoken to you are spirit and are life."** In biblical imagination, God's speech is never mere sound waves; it is life-breathing, reality-shaping, Spirit-carried action.

Carry that pattern forward, and you begin to notice how often sound precedes the sign. Joshua's people circle in silence, then trumpets blast and shouts rise—the walls of Jericho fall (see Joshua 6). David's harp soothes a tormented king—the oppressive spirit relents (see 1 Samuel 16). At midnight, Paul and Silas pray and sing—the prison shakes, chains drop, and hearts open (see Acts 16). At Pentecost, there is a sound from heaven—the church is born, and speech becomes a bridge not a barrier (see Acts 2). Even the Lord's cries from the cross and the loud voice that heralds His finished work carry a weight scripture won't let us ignore (see Matthew 27:46–50, John 19:30).

These scenes do not invite us to treat sound as a lever; they invite us to trust the Lord who moves when His people obey in worship. They also caution us. Israel could blow trumpets on command because God had spoken first. David's music was effective because he was God's man playing God's song in God's time. Paul and Silas were not working a technique; they were yielding to a Presence. The difference between manipulation and ministry is not the decibel level—it is the Lordship of Jesus and the fruit that remains.

Consider Babel and Pentecost together. At Babel, one language becomes a tool for self-exaltation—**"let us make a name for ourselves"**—and God mercifully confuses the project (see Genesis 11). At Pentecost, many languages become a miracle of proclamation— **"we hear... the mighty works of God"**—and God gathers the nations (see Acts 2). Unity divorced from obedience becomes dangerous power. Unity, drenched in the Spirit, becomes a holy witness. The church's "corporate sound" is safest and strongest when it is a response to God's self-disclosure, not an attempt to force His hand.

Angels, too, belong in this soundscape, not as curiosities but as coworkers sent to minister to the heirs of salvation (see Hebrews 1:14). Scripture shows them strengthening, announcing, guarding, executing God's purposes. Our task is not to command angels as if they were instruments in our studio; our task is to align with God's will so heaven's help can run on cleared tracks. The Spirit leads; the Word clarifies; worship humbles; obedience opens space.

Finally, a word on language like "frequency" and "vibration." Use it as a bridge, not a boundary. If by "frequency" we mean the moral-spiritual tenor of a life—the way speech, tone, posture, music, and emotion can either align with love or amplify fear— scripture has plenty to say. If by "frequency" we mean a secret technique that guarantees outcomes, scripture says no. The Lord is a person, not a principle. We walk with Him. We listen, we sing, we shout, we keep silence, we speak peace, we rebuke storms, we bless enemies and we look for a new creation to peek through.

PRACTICAL APPLICATION

Hover → Hear: Before you speak, post, or decide, go quiet: *"Holy Spirit, hover over this."* Listen, then move.

Sound-after-Word: Find one verse that fits today's situation (forgiveness, courage, patience). Speak a one-line confession from it, and take one matching step of obedience.

Jericho Rhythm: Pray silently over one "wall" for six days; on day seven, thank God aloud and serve someone affected by that wall (see Joshua 6).

David's Harp Practice: Play Christ-exalting worship when anxious (see 1 Samuel 16). Let praise steady your interior before you speak.

Pentecost, not Babel: With any group plan, ask: "Are we making *His* name known or ours?" If it's His, seek one-accord prayer before action (see Acts 2:1, 11).

Angel-Aware Alignment: Pray, *"Father, as I align with Your will, let Your angels minister as You desire"* (see Hebrews 1:14). Do **not** try to command them.

Corporate Linger: After singing, linger; then share a scripture-rooted declaration and a simple "Amen step" for the week.

REFLECTION QUESTIONS

1. Where are you tempted to use "sound" like a lever instead of yielding to Jesus' Lordship?

2. What decision this week needs *hovering first, obedience second*—and what verse anchors it?

3. Where has your community chased Babel-style unity (brand, hype) over Pentecost-style obedience?

4. Which "wall" are you circling in prayer, and what loving action fits day seven?

5. How can you translate "frequency/vibration" talk into scripture-shaped practices that exalt Jesus?

6. When have you felt God's help arrive as you aligned with His will (see Hebrews 1:14)?

7. What does faithful **silence** look like for you—and when must it turn into a faithful **shout**?

ACTIVATION PRAYER

Brooding Spirit, hover over my unformed places. Tune my heart to Your Word so my sound follows Your voice. Keep me from technique and teach me trust—silence when You say wait, a shout of thanks when You say move. Make my mouth a servant of Jesus' Lordship and my actions a witness to Your love. Form Pentecost in my community: unity that obeys, praise that builds a bridge, declarations that bear fruit. As I align with Your will, release every help You ordain—seen and unseen—for the sake of Your purposes. Let new creation peek through my worship, my obedience, and my words. In Jesus' name. Amen.

KEY TAKEAWAYS

1. **Genesis pattern:** Spirit hovers → God speaks → creation answers—our obedience fits that order.

2. **Sound follows the Word;** it's stewardship, not a shortcut or lever.

3. **Pentecost undoes Babel:** unity under the Spirit for God's fame, not ours.

4. **Worship steadies and opens space** for God's work; manipulation closes it.

5. **Angels minister as God wills;** our role is alignment, not command.

6. **Silence and shout** both belong—use the one the Spirit leads.

VERSE FOR MEDITATION

John 6:63 — "It is the Spirit who gives life; the flesh profits nothing. The words that I speak to you are spirit, and they are life." (NKJV).

Why it fits: It brings Word and Spirit together—the heartbeat of "brooding" that births new worlds.

POST THIS

"Brood, then obey—let sound follow the Word."
#DivineUnion #SpiritAndWord
#YouthEmpowerment #IncarnateLife #WalkItOut

Caption: *"Today I'm hovering before I speak. My 'Amen step':* _____*."*

CTA: Tag one friend and agree on a 60-second linger after worship this week.

CHAPTER 12

STEWARDING A HOLY SOUND IN ORDINARY DAYS

If in Him we live and move and have our being (see Acts 17:28), then ordinary hours are holy ground. The "sound" of a believer's life is not confined to microphones and sanctuaries. It is the timbre of a reconciled heart in a meeting. It is the cadence of patient words with a child. It is the hush of listening before speaking. It is the boldness to say "peace" into panic and "forgive" into fracture. Proverbs reminds us that life and death are in the power of the tongue; James warns us that blessing and cursing must not flow from the same mouth (see Proverbs 18:21, James 3:9–10). Stewardship begins there.

Worship teams and prayerful people should think musically and morally simultaneously. We honor the "new song" command not only by writing fresh lyrics but by offering the freshness of mercy, humility, and justice (see Psalm 96, Lamentations 3:22–23). We pay attention to atmospheres—does this set list serve love of God and neighbor, or does it chase an effect? We resist using predictable crescendos to get predictable reactions; instead, we ask for the Presence who transforms. A good diagnostic is Romans 12: after we sing, do we become more hospitable, more merciful, more diligent, more peaceable? If not, we made noise; we did not make disciples.

Emotion matters. Scripture never asks us to be emotionless; it asks us to be Spirit-led. In prayer and proclamation, emotion can energize truth or weaponize it. The psalms teach us to pour out our souls to God, then let God reorder the soul. In community, we learn to weep with those who weep and rejoice with those who rejoice (see Romans 12:15). A sanctified "vibration," if we keep the metaphor, is simply love-shaped emotion yoked to truth.

What about technology and the ocean of "healing frequencies" online? Use discernment. Music can comfort, calm, and even help our bodies settle; Scripture says so, and many of us have lived it. But neither playlists nor numbers in a video title are sacraments. Don't replace medical care with audio files, and don't outsource prayer to background noise.

If you choose to use instrumental ambience for study, rest, or devotions, do so with thanksgiving, Scripture open, and Jesus at the center.

Your body is a temple of the Holy Spirit. Steward sleep, movement, and food as worship, not superstition (see 1 Corinthians 6:19–20). Healthy rhythms help you notice God and neighbor. But greater than any regimen is a surrendered tongue and a softened heart. The "frequency" that most marks a son or daughter of God is mercy. Mercy sounds like Jesus. Mercy changes rooms. Mercy outlasts the year.

In this moment, imagine God pressing "reset" not to erase you but to re-tune you. If the world were handed back to the church and the Lord said, *"Build with Me,"* what kind of world would your words begin to frame? Romans 8 answers with a fierce benediction: nothing can separate us from the love of God in Christ Jesus our Lord. Start there. Speak from there. Sing from there. Go from there.

PRACTICAL APPLICATION

60-Second Hush: Before hard conversations or posts, pause one minute: *"Holy Spirit, set my tone."* Then speak briefly, truthfully, kindly (see Proverbs 18:21, James 3:9–10).

Mercy First Phrase: When tension rises, open with *"Peace to you"* or *"Please forgive me"* before any explanation (see Romans 12:18).

Romans 12 Diagnostic (after worship): Ask, *"Did our singing produce hospitality, mercy, diligence, peacemaking?"* If not, adjust next week's set + service plan.

Emotion Stewardship: Journal one strong emotion daily → pray a psalm line that names it → choose one loving action shaped by truth (see Romans 12:15).

Tech Discernment: If using "healing music," keep Jesus central: open scripture, give thanks, pray; never replace medical care or prayer with playlists.

Temple Triad (1 habit each): Sleep on purpose, move your body, eat with gratitude (see 1 Corinthians 6:19–20). Note how these tune your awareness of God and neighbor.

Blessing Routine: Speak the Aaronic blessing (see Numbers 6:24–26) over family/friends by name at breakfast or bedtime.

Weekly "Ordinary Sound" Audit: Track your words for a day (bless, curse, complain, encourage, listen). Replace one recurring negative with a practiced blessing and a matching deed.

REFLECTION QUESTIONS

1. Where do blessing and cursing still flow from the same mouth for you, and what practice will close that gap?

2. Does your worship planning serve love of God and neighbor—or chase an effect? What will you change this month?

3. Which everyday space (meeting, classroom, taxi, kitchen) most needs your reconciled tone?

4. How have you used emotion to **energize** truth—or to **weaponize** it? What does Spirit-led emotion look like for you?

5. What "frequency" habits (music, ambience) help you focus on Jesus—and which distract you?

6. If God pressed "reset," what world would your words start framing this week?

ACTIVATION PRAYER

Father, in You I live and move and have my being. Tune my heart and tongue to Your mercy. Holy Spirit, lead my emotions, steady my tone, and make my speech a servant of love and truth. Let my worship produce Romans 12 fruit—hospitality, diligence, generosity, mercy, and peace. Guard me from manipulating atmospheres; teach me to welcome Your Presence with humility and obedience. Help me steward my body as Your temple so I'm attentive to You and useful to my neighbors. Set my ordinary hours apart: meetings, chores, messages, and meals. From Your unbreakable love in Christ, let my words bless, my silences heal, and my actions agree with what I say. In Jesus' name. Amen.

KEY TAKEAWAYS

1. **Ordinary hours are holy ground;** your daily tone is your ministry.

2. **Worship must yield Romans 12 fruit,** not just feelings.

3. **Emotion matters—Spirit-led, love-shaped, truth-yoked.**

4. **Speech is stewardship, not magic;** bless more than you explain.

5. **Use tech/music with discernment;** Jesus stays central.

6. **Mercy is the believer's defining "frequency."**

VERSE FOR MEDITATION

Romans 8:38–39 — "For I am persuaded that neither death nor life... shall be able to separate us from the love of God which is in Christ Jesus our Lord." (NKJV).

Why it fits: Your daily sound should flow from this unshakeable love—start here, speak from here.

POST THIS

"Mercy is my frequency—everyday, everywhere."
#DivineUnion #PracticeHisPresence #Romans12Life
#SpeakLife #YouthEmpowerment #WalkItOut

Caption: *"Today's mercy move:* _____.
Who needs a blessing from my mouth?"

CTA: Tag one person you'll bless by name today and drop a one-sentence blessing in the comments.

CHAPTER 13

THE UNSHAKABLE KINGDOM WITHIN

"Therefore, since we are receiving a kingdom which cannot be shaken, let us have grace." (Hebrews 12:28 - NKJV).

The book of Hebrews pulls back the curtain on Jesus—our High Priest, our once-for-all sacrifice, our forerunner—and invites us to live from a different center. The writer closes with a startling vision: *everything that can be shaken will be shaken, yet the kingdom we have received in Christ remains unshakable* (see Hebrews 12:26–29). That is more than a doctrine. It is a way to stand, think, love, and run our race.

The race is personal. **"Let us lay aside every weight, and the sin which so easily ensnares us, and let us run...looking unto Jesus."** (Hebrews 12:1–2 - NKJV). Scripture refuses to shrink sin down to a few notorious behaviors. **"Whatever is not from faith is sin." (Romans 14:23 - NKJV).** Disobedience blocks momentum. Trust unlocks it. You were not called to sprint someone else's lane. You were summoned to run yours with perseverance. Paul could say without flinching, **"I have finished the race." (2 Timothy 4:7 - NKJV).** That confidence did not come from a trouble-free path. It grew from a clear gaze.

Fixing our eyes on Jesus is not pious window dressing. It is a practical reorientation. Many of us habitually project unwanted futures and then live today under the weight of the worlds we imagined. The apostle gives us a healthier script: **"Whatever is true, whatever is honorable, whatever is just, whatever is pure... think about these things" (Philippians 4:8 - ESV).** Faith looks ahead and borrows tomorrow's joy. **"I consider that the sufferings of this present time are not worth comparing with the glory that will be revealed in us" (Romans 8:18 - TPT).** Jesus endured the cross **"for the joy set before Him." (Hebrews 12:2 - NASB).**

Hope is not denial. Hope is sight. When anxiety spikes, close your eyes and behold Christ with the eyes of your heart. **"You will keep him in perfect peace, whose mind is stayed on You." (Isaiah 26:3 - NKJV).** Cast every care on Him, because He cares for you (see 1 Peter 5:7).

Hebrews names the company we keep while we run. We are **"surrounded by so great a cloud of witnesses" (Hebrews 12:1 - NKJV)**—the men and women of chapter 11 whose testimony still speaks. They do not invite us to chase mystical experiences or attempt to contact the dead, which Scripture forbids (see Deuteronomy 18:10–12). Their lives encourage us to finish ours. **"All these... did not receive what was promised, since God had provided something better for us, so that apart from us they would not be made perfect." (Hebrews 11:39–40 - NASB).** The story reaches its completion as the people of God, across generations, are brought to maturity together in Christ. We honor that cloud best by staying faithful in the lane we have been given.

The author then lifts our eyes higher still:

"You have come to Mount Zion and to the city of the living God, the heavenly Jerusalem, and to innumerable angels in festal gathering, and to the assembly of the firstborn who are enrolled in heaven, and to God, the Judge of all, and to the spirits of the righteous made perfect, and to Jesus,

the mediator of a new covenant, and to the sprinkled blood that speaks better than the blood of Abel." (Hebrews 12:22–24 - ESV/NASB blend).

This is the landscape of the unshakable kingdom. Dallas Willard described the kingdom as *the range of God's effective will*—the realm where what God wants done is done. Jesus announced that kingdom and then placed it startlingly near. **"The kingdom of God is within you." (Luke 17:21 - NKJV)**, or **"in your midst" (NASB)**. The King lives in you, and you live in His kingdom. You are more than a person trying hard to be religious. You are a Spirit-indwelt temple (see 1 Corinthians 3:16), a citizen of heaven (see Philippians 3:20), a living stone in a house God is building (see 1 Peter 2:5). The company listed in Hebrews 12 is not far away. Heaven's realities press in on the church's ordinary life.

Discernment matters when that world brushes ours. Test the spirits to see whether they are from God (see 1 John 4:1). Do not label every unusual moment demonic by default. Do not swallow every impression untested. The Spirit's ministry will magnify Jesus, align with scripture, and produce the fruit of love, joy, peace, and holiness (see John 16:14, Galatians 5:22–23, Hebrews 12:14).

The letter also reminds us that the God who welcomes is the God who purifies. **"Our God is a consuming fire." (Hebrews 12:29 - NKJV).** Fire in scripture refines more often than it destroys. **"He will sit as a refiner and purifier of silver." (Malachi 3:3 - NKJV).** Trials prove faith **"more precious than gold." (1 Peter 1:7 - NKJV).** John the Baptist promised that Christ would baptize His people **"with the Holy Spirit and fire." (Matthew 3:11 - NKJV).** Sanctification is that gracious, ongoing work where the Spirit burns away what cannot remain, and Christ's likeness emerges. Job understood it: **"When He has tested me, I shall come forth as gold." (Job 23:10 - NKJV).**

Creation's ache is part of this story. Paul says the whole creation groans, longing for the revealing of the sons and daughters of God (see Romans 8:19–22). Humanity was made to bear God's image and steward God's world. The fall fractured that vocation. Technology and tools can be gifts, yet they cannot replace the restored life God is forming in us through Christ. Redemption is not only about getting souls to heaven. God is reconciling all things to Himself in Christ (see Colossians 1:20), summing up everything in Him (see Ephesians 1:10). Christ in you remains **"the hope of glory." (Colossians 1:27 - NKJV).**

One line from the early church has helped many: *"God became man that man might become god."* Athanasius did not mean we become divine by nature. He meant we are invited to share in God's life by grace. Scripture says we become **"partakers of the divine nature." (2 Peter 1:4 - NKJV).** The Son took on our humanity so we could share His life, righteousness, and fellowship with the Father through the Spirit. That is the heart behind every summons in Hebrews—to draw near with confidence, to receive mercy, to find grace, to live holy because we are held (see Hebrews 4:16; 12:14).

Hebrews 13 lands this theology in everyday love. Keep loving one another as family. Show hospitality; some have entertained angels without knowing it (see Hebrews 13:1–2). Remember prisoners as though chained with them, and honor marriage. Live free from the love of money.

Let your conduct be without covetousness; be content with such things as you have. For He Himself has said, "I will never leave you nor forsake you." (Hebrews 13:5 - NKJV).

Jesus Christ is the same yesterday, today, and forever. (Hebrews 13:8 -NKJV).

Through Him then, let's continually offer up a sacrifice of praise to God, that is, the fruit of lips praising His name. And do not neglect doing good and sharing, for with such sacrifices God is pleased. (Hebrews 13:15–16 - NASB).

Obey your leaders and submit to them—for they keep watch over your souls as those who will give an account—so that they may do this with joy, not groaning; for this would be unhelpful for you. Pray for us, for we are sure that we have a good conscience, desiring to conduct ourselves honorably in all things. (Hebrews 13:17–18 - NASB).

The benediction is a banner over our lives:

Now may the God of peace who brought again from the dead our Lord Jesus, the great shepherd of the sheep, by the blood of the eternal covenant, equip you with everything good that you may do his will, working in us that which is pleasing in his sight, through Jesus Christ, to whom be glory forever and ever. Amen. (Hebrews 13:20–21 - ESV).

Two pastoral clarifications may help young disciples who are eager and curious. First, learn from the saints who have gone before us without trying to summon them. Their witness cheers us on; their finished race proves God keeps covenant; their faith feeds ours (see Hebrews 12:1). Second, dream boldly while rooting every practice in scripture and the character of Jesus. Faith is not magic. Faith is fidelity to a faithful God. Jesus taught us to ask, believe, and receive (see Mark 11:24), yet He also taught us to pray, **"Your will be done." (Matthew 6:10 - NKJV).** Mature faith holds both, trusting the Father's heart even when outcomes differ from our expectations.

Gaze at Jesus until your imagination is baptized in hope. Guard your inner world; refuse to seed your future with fear. Welcome the presence of God's kingdom within you and among your community. Practice the basics of Hebrews 13 with stubborn joy: brotherly love, open doors, compassionate remembrance, sexual faithfulness, contentment, grateful worship, and generous sharing. Discern the Spirit's work and cooperate with the Spirit's fire. Run your race. Finish well.

"The One who calls you is faithful, and He will do it." (1 Thessalonians 5:24 - NIV).

PRACTICAL APPLICATION

Unshakable Morning Litany: Pray Hebrews 12:28— **"I'm receiving an unshakable kingdom; I choose grace today."** Add Isaiah 26:3 and 1 Peter 5:7.

Lane Check: Name one *"weight"* and one *"sin that entangles"* (see Hebrews 12:1). Drop the weight (boundary or action). Confess the sin. Replace both with one faithful step.

Gaze → Run (daily cue): When anxiety spikes, close your eyes for 30 seconds: *Look to Jesus* (see Hebrews 12:2). Then take the **smallest next obedience**.

Fire-to-Gold Test: In a current trial, write: *What is being burned away? What Christlike gold is forming?* (see Malachi 3:3, 1 Peter 1:7).

Zion Awareness Pause: Once today, read Hebrews 12:22–24 aloud. Thank Jesus, then bless your workplace or home with one Romans 12 deed.

Hebrews 13 Workout (one per day): Brotherly love • Hospitality • Remember the marginalized • Honor marriage • Contentment • Sacrifice of praise • Do good and share.

Discernment Guardrails: For any unusual impression:

1. Scripture-align?
2. Jesus-exalting?
3. Fruit of the Spirit?

If "no" anywhere—pause and seek counsel (see 1 John 4:1, Galatians 5:22–23).

REFLECTION QUESTIONS

1. What "weights" feel respectable but slow your race, and what boundary will you set this week?

2. Where is your gaze fixed by default—news, fears, rivals, or Jesus? How will you retrain it daily?

3. Which part of Hebrews 13 is most underdeveloped in you, and what micro-practice will grow it?

4. How is God's refining fire meeting you right now, and what gold is He forming?

5. When have you mistaken adrenaline for faith? What does **grace-fueled perseverance** look like today?

6. How can you honor the "cloud of witnesses" without chasing experiences scripture forbids?

7. Where do you see creation "groaning," and what faithful act of stewardship or mercy fits your lane?

ACTIVATION PRAYER

God of peace, thank You that I am receiving a kingdom that cannot be shaken. Fix my eyes on Jesus—the author and finisher of my faith. By Your Spirit, help me lay aside every weight and the sin that entangles, and run with perseverance the race marked out for me. Refine me with holy fire; burn away what cannot remain and form Christ's likeness in me. Anchor my heart in Your nearness—Mount Zion, the blood that speaks better things, the fellowship of Your people. Equip me with everything good to do Your will today; make my lips offer praise and my hands do good and share. Keep me steady in shaking, content in Your care, and courageous in love. In Jesus' name. Amen.

KEY TAKEAWAYS

1. You're **receiving** (present tense) an **unshakable kingdom**—stand in grace (see Hebrews 12:28).

2. **Gaze precedes pace:** look to Jesus, then run your lane (see Hebrews 12:1–2).

3. God's **fire refines** sons and daughters into gold, not ash (see Malachi 3:3, 1 Peter 1:7).

4. The kingdom is **within/in your midst**—live Zion awareness in ordinary places (see Luke 17:21, Hebrews 12:22–24).

5. **Discern everything:** Spirit-led, scripture-aligned, Jesus-exalting, fruit-producing.

6. Hebrews 13 turns doctrine into **daily love**—hospitality, contentment, praise, generosity, and integrity.

VERSE FOR MEDITATION

Hebrews 12:28 — "Therefore, since we are receiving a kingdom which cannot be shaken, let us have grace..." (NKJV).

Why it fits: It is the chapter's center of gravity—security that empowers holy living.

POST THIS

"Unshakable within—run your lane with grace."
#DivineUnion #Hebrews12 #UnshakableKingdom
#RunYourRace #YouthEmpowerment #WalkItOut

Caption: *"Today's weight I'm dropping: _____.*
Smallest next obedience: _____."

CTA: Tag one friend to join you in the Hebrews 13 Workout this week.

CHAPTER 14

THE STILL SMALL VOICE

"What is man that You are mindful of him, and the son of man that You visit him? For You have made him a little lower than Elohim, and You have crowned him with glory and honor. You have made him to have dominion over the works of Your hands; You have put all things under his feet." (Psalm 8:4–6 - NKJV).

Psalm 8 sketches God's original intention for humanity, and Hebrews echoes it, applying the psalm to Jesus and to those united with Him (see Hebrews 2:5–10). Redemption is not merely rescue from sin; redemption restores us to purposeful, Spirit-filled stewardship under Christ. We have been "raised up together, and made to sit together in the heavenly places in Christ Jesus." (Ephesians 2:6 - NKJV). If we are already seated with Him, the goal of the Christian life is not *get to heaven someday,*" but grow up into Christ today. The Spirit aims at transformation—of mind, desires, habits, relationships, and even how we engage creation (see Romans 12:1–2, Colossians 3:1–4).

Scripture assumes a real spiritual world and a real physical world. Mature disciples learn to live faithfully in both without denying either. Elijah met God not in wind, earthquake, or fire, but in *"a gentle and quiet whisper"* (see 1 Kings 19:12). Jesus said, **"My sheep hear My voice, and I know them, and they follow Me." (John 10:27 - NKJV).** Paul adds, **"The mature children of God are those who are moved by the impulses of the Holy Spirit." (Romans 8:14 - TPT).** Guidance often begins with what many of us have called the *"still small voice."*

Dallas Willard wrote, *"Hearing God is not a freakish experience; it is a conversational relationship with our living Lord."* That quiet inner nudge will never contradict scripture, never diminish Jesus, and never produce the works of the flesh. It tends to carry the aroma of James 3 wisdom—**"pure, peace-loving, considerate, submissive, full of mercy." (James 3:17 - NIV).**

That voice shaped my life. I once carried the words *"worthless"* and *"not enough"* like name tags. God met me in ordinary days and invited me to take small, obedient risks: *Write what I give you. Learn what you do not yet know. Serve people. Keep saying yes.* Skills were learned from scratch, doors opened unexpectedly, and a vocation emerged that I had not imagined. None of that makes me special. It does prove that steady obedience to the Spirit's promptings can reorder a life. **"Commit your works to the Lord and your thoughts will be established." (Proverbs 16:3 - NKJV).**

Young people often ask, *"How do I know this inner voice is from God?"* Use a simple, biblical filter.

1. **Scripture:** God's voice harmonizes with God's Word (see 2 Timothy 3:16–17).

2. **Christlikeness:** The Spirit magnifies Jesus and produces His character (see John 16:14, Galatians 5:22–23).

3. **Counsel:** Wisdom welcomes correction and community confirmation (see Proverbs 11:14).

4. **Fruit and peace:** God's guidance bears good fruit over time and is accompanied by the peace of Christ ruling in the heart (see Colossians 3:15).

5. **Humility:** Hold impressions with open hands. Use soft language when you are learning. *"I sense..."* is safer than *"God told me..."* while you test and grow (see 1 John 4:1).

Job 38–39 reminds us that God sustains the vastness and intricacy of creation. Humanity's calling is not to seize divine prerogatives but to image God's wise rule within our creaturely limits. Stewardship was always our lane (see Genesis 1:26–28). Creation now "groans" under futility, waiting for the revealing of mature sons and daughters who live under the Spirit's leadership (see Romans 8:19–22). Read the poetry of Job, Psalms, and Proverbs with reverence. Much of the language points to Christ, **"the power of God and the wisdom of God" (1 Corinthians 1:24 - NKJV).** Treat personified images, such as "Goodness and Mercy" in Psalm 23, as the Spirit's way of assuring us that God's covenant love pursues His people, rather than as independent beings to be sought after.

Balance matters. A hunger for spiritual realities must be matched by integrity in ordinary responsibilities. Many of us have prayed for miracles to erase the consequences of unwise patterns. Scripture calls that moment a chance to become teachable. **"If any of you lacks wisdom, let him ask of God... and it will be given to him." (James 1:5 - NKJV).** Care for the body God gave you. **"Or do you not know that your body is the temple of the Holy Spirit... therefore glorify God in your body." (1 Corinthians 6:19–20 - NKJV).** You cannot binge on processed foods and then expect a miracle when the body goes awry. Choose food and rhythms that serve health. Train, because **"bodily exercise profits a little"** and self-control is a fruit of the Spirit (see 1 Timothy 4:8, Galatians 5:23). Seek medical counsel when needed, pray for healing, and keep walking wisely. Miracles do not excuse negligence; grace empowers stewardship.

Fear is a frequent barrier to spiritual growth. Scripture is explicit: **"God has not given us a spirit of fear, but of power and of love and of a sound mind." (2 Timothy 1:7 - NKJV).** Perfect love drives out the fear that punishes and paralyzes (see 1 John 4:18). Take fear seriously by taking small, courageous steps. Name the fear. Expose it to truth. Invite trusted friends to pray with you. Practice obedience in low-risk spaces and let courage grow.

Comparison also cripples. Jesus' word to Peter when he glanced sideways at John still stands: **"What is that to you? You follow Me." (John 21:22 - NKJV).** Each of us carries a unique assignment and a unique pace. Celebrate the graces others carry and stay true to your own path.

"Let each one examine his own work... for each one shall bear his own load." (Galatians 6:4–5 - NKJV).

Wisdom welcomes lifelong learning. Solomon personifies Wisdom in Proverbs 8, calling at the crossroads and city gates. That voice finds its fullness in Christ, **"in whom are hidden all the treasures of wisdom and knowledge." (Colossians 2:3 - NKJV).** Remain teachable. Read widely. Ask questions. Listen well, even to the young and the overlooked. **"Give instruction to a wise man, and he will be still wiser." (Proverbs 9:9 - NKJV).**

Here is a simple rule of life for those who want to live in divine union with Jesus in their everyday lives:

✓ **Choose awareness.** Practice the presence of God throughout your day. Whisper often, *"Speak, Lord; Your servant is listening"* (see 1 Samuel 3:9).

✓ **Choose obedience.** Respond quickly to small promptings. Faithfulness in little becomes faithfulness in much (see Luke 16:10).

✓ **Choose holiness.** Welcome the Spirit's refining fire. God's fire purifies what cannot last and strengthens what must remain (see Hebrews 12:28–29, Malachi 3:3).

✓ **Choose love.** Keep Hebrews 13 near at hand: brotherly love, hospitality, compassion, sexual integrity, contentment, grateful worship, generous sharing, humble submission, fervent prayer (see Hebrews 13:1–18).

✓ **Choose hope.** Seed your future with God's promises rather than your fears. **"You will keep him in perfect peace, whose mind is stayed on You." (Isaiah 26:3 - NKJV).**

A.W. Tozer once said, *"The voice of God is a friendly voice."* That line has become a plumb line for me. The

Shepherd's voice leads, cleanses, corrects, and dignifies. It may confront, yet it never condemns those in Christ. It may stretch you, yet it will not shame you. Follow that voice. Test it by the Word. Confirm it in community. Watch for its fruit.

"Beloved, I pray that in every way you may succeed and prosper and be in good health, just as your soul prospers." (3 John 2 - AMP).

"Faithful is He who calls you, and He also will bring it to pass." (1 Thessalonians 5:24 - NASB).

PRACTICAL APPLICATION

Whisper Minute: Breathe, then pray: *"Speak, Lord; Your servant is listening"* (see 1 Samuel 3:9). Note the nudge; obey one small step.

S.C.C.F.H. Discernment (use before acting):

- ✓ Scripture-align?
- ✓ Christlike?
- ✓ Counsel welcomed?
- ✓ Fruit and peace evident?
- ✓ Humility in tone?

(If any "no," pause.)

Whisper Journal: Date, *what I sensed, verse that anchors it, counsel I sought, fruit/outcome.* Review weekly.

Fear → Faith Swap: Name one fear; confess 2 Timothy 1:7 aloud; take one low-risk obedience that contradicts the fear.

Comparison Fast (24 hrs): Mute one feed that triggers envy. Repeat Jesus' word: *"You follow Me"* (John 21:22). Do one gratitude act for your lane.

Temple Tune-Up: Steward body as worship (see 1 Corinthians 6:19–20)—sleep on purpose, move 15 minutes, eat with gratitude. Notice clearer hearing when rested.

Integrity First: For any *"miracle ask,"* pair a wisdom action: book the appointment, apologize, budget, study (see James 1:5, Proverbs 16:3).

James-3 Filter for Tone: Before speaking, ask: *Is it pure, peace-loving, considerate, full of mercy?* (see James 3:17). If not, rewrite it.

REFLECTION QUESTIONS

1. Which cue helps you notice the Shepherd's voice fastest, and when do you ignore it?

2. Where have you used *"God told me"* language when you should have said *"I sense..."*? What will you correct?

3. What fear most blocks your obedience right now, and what is a small, faithful counter-step?

4. How can you match spiritual hunger with ordinary integrity this week (study, work, money, health)?

5. When did comparison steal your joy? What boundary or habit will protect your lane?

6. Which recent impression passed scripture or Christlikeness but failed peace orfruit? What does that teach you?

7. How will you invite community counsel without outsourcing your responsibility to obey?

ACTIVATION PRAYER

Jesus, Good Shepherd, teach me Your still small voice. Tune my heart to Your Word so that what I "hear" never contradicts scripture and always magnifies You. Holy Spirit, replace fear with power, love, and a sound mind. Grow in me James-3 wisdom—pure, peaceable, gentle, full of mercy. Give me humility to test impressions, courage to obey small prompts, and patience to wait when You are silent. Purify my desires; refine me with holy fire. Help me steward my body, my time, and my words as worship. Guard me from comparison and condemnation; anchor me in Your friendly voice that leads and dignifies. Establish my thoughts as I commit my works to You. In Jesus' name. Amen.

KEY TAKEAWAYS

1. God's "still small voice" never contradicts scripture, diminishes Jesus, or produces fleshly works.

2. Discern with **Scripture, Christlikeness, Counsel, Fruit and Peace, Humility**—then obey.

3. Miracles don't excuse negligence; grace empowers wise stewardship of ordinary responsibilities.

4. Fear and comparison distort guidance; love and lane-faithfulness clarify it.

5. Awareness, obedience, holiness, love, and hope form a simple, lifelong rule of life.

VERSE FOR MEDITATION

1 Kings 19:12 — "… a still small voice." (NKJV).

Why it fits: The chapter centers on learning the Shepherd's gentle guidance over the noise.

POST THIS

"Follow the whisper—test it, then obey."
#DivineUnion #StillSmallVoice #ChristInMe
#YouthEmpowerment #PracticeHisPresence
#WalkItOut

Caption: *"Today's whisper → step:* _____.
Verse anchoring it: _____."

CTA: Tag a friend who can lovingly T.E.S.T. your next step with you this week.

CONCLUSION

The way of Jesus is wonderfully ordinary and wonderfully supernatural. The Shepherd still speaks, and His people still learn to recognize His voice in the hum of daily life (see John 10:27). Quiet nudges become decisive turns when they are tested by scripture, confirmed in community, and obeyed with a willing heart. This is not elitism or escapism; it is the normal Christian life—rooted in the Word, centered on Christ, and animated by the Spirit.

Maturity looks like balance. Disciples honor both the unseen and the seen, cultivating prayer and presence with God while stewarding bodies, time, relationships, and work. Miracles remain God's gracious prerogative, yet wisdom invites better choices, healthier rhythms, and faithful habits. **"Let the peace of Christ rule in your hearts"** becomes a daily governor, not a rare exception (see Colossians 3:15).

Fear loses ground where love is practiced. The Spirit trains courage in small obediences, and those obediences compound into a life of holy audacity. Perfection is not the requirement; responsiveness is. Faithfulness in little remains God's chosen path to faithfulness in much (see Luke 16:10).

Comparison has no place here. Each assignment is tailored; each pace is kind. Celebrate the graces of others while staying attentive to the voice that addresses you by name. **"Trust in the Lord with all your heart... and He shall direct your paths" (Proverbs 3:5–6 - NKJV).** The will of God is not a maze to get lost in; it is a relationship to walk out.

Keep your future seeded with promise rather than fear. Lift your gaze to the unshakable kingdom that already resides within by the Spirit, and let your speech, imagination, and planning agree with it (see Hebrews 12:28–29). Gratitude and generosity tune the heart to heaven's frequency; hospitality and holiness keep the door open for God's presence.

This is the invitation: *live awake to God, listen for the still small voice, test what you hear, and move with humility and hope.*

Faithful is He who calls you, and He also will do it. (1 Thessalonians 5:24 - NASB).

30-DAY PRACTICE PLAN

DAYS 1–7: PRESENCE

- Read Hebrews 12:22–29 daily.
- Two minutes of silence after reading.
- One hidden act of service.

DAYS 8–14: LISTENING

- Read John 10:1–10 daily.
- Journal one line: *"Today I sensed Jesus leading me to..."*
- Share one decision with a mentor for feedback.

DAYS 15–21: OBEDIENCE

- Read Colossians 3:12–17 daily.
- Practice the discernment triad (Bible, counsel, peace) for one choice.
- Replace one complaint each day with a short prayer of blessing.

DAYS 22–30: WITNESS

- Read Philippians 2:1–11 daily.
- Invite a friend to church or youth group.
- Tell one *"kingdom moment"* story to your small group.

CLOSING BENEDICTION

May the God of peace equip you with everything good to do His will.

May Christ dwell richly in you—mind renewed, tongue sanctified, hands ready.

May your home be a seedbed of mercy; your speech, a servant of love; your work, worship.

Go in the name of Jesus—carrying the unshakable kingdom into every street. Amen.

(Ref: Hebrews 13:20–21, Colossians 3:16, Romans 12:1–2)

www.ingramcontent.com/pod-product-compliance
Lightning Source LLC
Chambersburg PA
CBHW021110130626
46554CB00002B/613